Donald Grant Mitchell

Bound together: a sheaf of papers

Donald Grant Mitchell
Bound together: a sheaf of papers
ISBN/EAN: 9783743328426
Manufactured in Europe, USA, Canada, Australia, Japa
Cover: Foto ©ninafisch / pixelio.de

Manufactured and distributed by brebook publishing software (www.brebook.com)

Donald Grant Mitchell

Bound together: a sheaf of papers

BOUND TOGETHER.

By DON^D G. MITCHELL.

BOUND TOGETHER:

A

SHEAF OF PAPERS

BY THE AUTHOR OF
"WET DAYS AT EDGEWOOD," REVERIES OF
A BACHELOR," ETC.

NEW YORK
CHARLES SCRIBNER'S SONS
1893

PREFATORY NOTE.

TWO or three of the papers contained in this volume have already appeared in print; the others are new to type, though some of them may date back a half dozen years, or more. I wish they were fresher; I wish they were better. Yet they contain things which seemed to me true and worth saying, when they first came to my pen; and which, now that I re-read them, seem still to be true; else, I would not say them again.

The book is a medley, in which the grandiloquence of open-air speech is set beside the easy familiarities of the chimney corner. But what more could be looked for in a Sheaf of Papers for which I could find — after considerable search — no more unifying title, than to say they are *BOUND TOGETHER?*

D. G. M.

EDGEWOOD, March, 1884.

CONTENTS.

	PAGE
I. WASHINGTON IRVING, 1783–1883,	3
II. TITIAN AND HIS TIMES,	19
III. PROCESSION OF THE MONTHS,	59
AMONG THE SNOWS,	61
SPRING-TIDE,	79
OLD FOURTH AND FRUITS,	98
PLAYTIME, PLAYS, AND PLANTING,	115
IV. BEGINNINGS OF AN OLD TOWN,	135
NORWICH, 1659–1859,	137
CENTENNIAL ADDRESS,	139
V. TWO COLLEGE TALKS,	161
FIRST TALK,	163
SECOND TALK,	192

CONTENTS.

	PAGE
VI. IN-DOORS AND OUT OF DOORS,	205
FIRES AND FIRESIDE,	207
HIGHWAYS AND PARKS,	228
HOUSE INTERIORS,	252
HOMES AND HOLIDAYS,	27.

WASHINGTON IRVING.

*Address at the Tarrytown Centennial Celebration
April 3, 1883.*

YOU are met to-night to pay tribute to the memory of a man we all loved — born a hundred years ago.

Yet, we who put voice to your tribute are brought to pause at the very start: Who can say over again — in a way that shall make listeners — the praises of a balmy day in June?

Simply to recall him however is — I think — to honor him: for there is no memory of him however shadowy or vagrant which is not grateful to you, — to me and to all the reading world.

It is now well nigh upon thirty-five years since I first met Mr. Irving: It was in a sunny parlor in one of the houses of that Colonnade Row which stands opposite the Astor Library in Lafayette Place,

New York. I can recall vividly the trepidation which I carried to that meeting — so eager to encounter the man whom all honored and admired: — so apprehensive lest a chilling dignity might disturb my ideal. And when that smiling, quiet, well-preserved gentleman (I could hardly believe him sixty-five) left his romp with some of his little kinsfolk, to give me a hearty shake of the hand, and thereafter to run on in lively humorsome chat — stealing all trepidation out of one, by — I know not what — kindly magnetism of voice and manner, it was as if some one were playing counterfeit: — as if the venerated author were yet to appear and displace this beaming, winning personality, with some awful dignity that should put me again into worshipful tremor.

But no: this was indeed Mr. Irving — hard as it was to adjust this gracious presence so full of benignity, with the author who had told the story of the Knickerbockers and of Columbus.

Another puzzle to me was — how this easy-going gentleman, with his winning mildness and quiet deliberation — as if he never *could*, and never *did*, and never *would* knuckle down to hard task-work — should have reeled out those hundreds — nay thousands of pages of graceful, well-ordered, sparkling English.

I could not understand how he did it. I do not

think we ever altogether understand how the birds sing and sing; and yet, with feathers quite unruffled, and eyes always a-twinkle.

My next sight of Mr. Irving was hereabout, at his own home. By his kind invitation I had come up to pass a day with him at Sunnyside, and he had promised me a drive through Sleepy Hollow.

What a promise that was! No boy ever went to his Christmas Holidays more joyously I think, than I, to meet that engagement.

It was along this road, beside which we are assembled to-night that we drove. He all alert and brisk, with the cool morning breeze blowing down upon us from over Haverstraw heights and across the wide sweep of River.

He called attention to the spot of poor André's capture — not forbearing that little touch of sympathy, which came to firmer, yet not disloyal expression, afterward, in his story of Washington. A sweep of his whip-hand told me the trees under which Paulding and the rest chanced to be loitering on that memorable day.

We were whirling along the same road a short way farther northward, when I ventured a query about the memorable night-ride of Ichabod Crane and of the Headless Horseman.

Aye, it was thereabout, that tragedy came off too.

"Down this bit of road the old horse 'Gunpowder' came thundering: there away — Brom Bones with his Pumpkin (I tell you this in confidence," he said) "was in waiting; and along here they went clattering neck and neck — Ichabod holding a good seat till Van Ripper's saddle-girths gave way, and then bumping and jouncing from side to side as he clung to mane or neck, (a little pantomime with the whip making it real) and so at last — away yonder — well, where you like, the poor pedagogue went sprawling to the ground — I hope in a soft place." And I think the rollicking humor of it was as much enjoyed by him that autumn morning, and that he felt in his bones just as relishy a smack of it all — as if Katrina Van Tassel had held her quilting frolic only on the yester-night.

Irving first came to know Tarrytown and Sleepy Hollow, when a boy of fourteen or fifteen — he passing some holidays in these parts, I think with his friend Paulding. To those days belong much of that idle sauntering along brooksides hereabout — with fly-books and fish-rods, and memories of Walton, which get such delightful recognition in a certain paper of the Sketch-Book.

Then, too, he with his companions came to know the old Dutch farmers of the region — whose home interiors found their way afterwards into his books.

I think he pointed out also, with a significant twinkle of the eye, which the dullest boy would have understood, some orchards, with which he had early acquaintance: and specially too — upon some hill-top (which I think I could find now) a farmery, famous for its cider mill and the good cider made there: — he, with the rest — testing it over and over in the old slow way with straws — but provoked once on a time to a fuller test, by turning the hogshead, so they might sip from the open bung; and then (whether out of mischief or mishandling, he did not absolutely declare to me) the big barrel got the better of them, and set off upon a lazy roll down the hill — going faster and faster — they, more and more frightened, and scudding away slant-wise over the fences — the yelling farmer appearing suddenly at the top of the slope, but too broad in the beam for any sharp race, and the hogshead between them plunging, and bounding, and giving out ghostly, guttural explosions of sound, and cider, at every turn.

You may judge if Mr. Irving did not put a nice touch to that story!

After this memorable autumn drive amongst the hills, I met with Mr. Irving frequently at his own home; and shall I be thought impertinent and indiscreet if I say, that at times — rare times it is true — I have seen this most amiable gentleman manifest a little of that restive choler which sometime flamed up in William the Testy: — not long-lived, not deliberate — but a little human blaze of impatience at something gone awry in the dressing of a garden border, in care of some stable-pet — that was all gone with the first blaze, but marked and indicated the sources of that wrathy and pious zest (with which he is not commonly credited) and with which he loved to put a contemptuous thrust of his sharper language into the bloat of upstart pride, and of conceit, and of insolent pretension.

The boy-mischief in him — which led him out from his old home in William Street — after hours — over the shed-roof, lingered in him for a good while, I think, and lent not a little point to some of the keener pictures of the Knickerbocker history: and if I do not mistake, there was now and then a quiet chuckle, as he told me of the foolish indignation with which some descendants of the old Dutch worthies had seen their ancestors put to a tender broil over the playful blaze of his humor.

Indeed there was a spontaneity and heartiness about that Knickerbocker history, which I think he carried a strong liking for, all his life.

The Sketch-Book, written years later, and when necessity enforced writing, was done with a great audience in his eye; and he won it, and keeps it bravely. I know there is a disposition to speak of it rather patronizingly and apologetically — as if it were reminiscent — Anglican — conventional — as if he would have done better if he had possessed our modern critical bias — or if he had been born in Boston — or born a philosopher outright: Well, perhaps so — perhaps so!

But I love to think and believe that our dear, old Mr. Irving was born just where he should have been born, and wrote in a way that it is hardly worth our while to try and mend for him.

I understand that a great many promising young people — without the fear of the critics before their eyes — keep on, persistently reading that old Sketch-Book, with its "Broken Hearts," and "Wife" twining like a vine, and "Spectre Bridegroom," and all the rest.

And there are old people I know, — one I am sure of — who never visit St. Paul's churchyard without wanting to peep over Irving's shoulders into Mr. Newbury's shop, full of dear old toy-books; — who never go to Stratford upon Avon but there is a hunt — first of all — for the Red Horse Tavern and the poker which was Irving's sceptre; — never a sail on summer afternoons past the wall of the blue Katskills, but there is a longing lookout for the stray cloud-caps, and an eager listening for the rumbling of the balls which thundered in the ears of poor Rip Van Winkle.

What, pray, if the hero of Bracebridge Hall be own cousin to Sir Roger de Coverley? Is that a relationship to be discarded? And could any other than the writer we honor, carry on more wisely the record of the cousinship, or with so sure a hand and so deft a touch, declare and establish our inheritance in the rural beatitudes of England?

It may be true that as we read some of those earlier books of his, we shall come upon some truisms which in these fast-paced times may chafe us — some rhetorical furbelows or broidery, that belong to the wardrobes of the past — some tears that flow too easily — but scarce ever a page anywhere, but on a sudden some shimmer of buoyant humor, breaks through all the crevices of a sentence — a humor not born of Rhetoric or measurable by critic's rules — but coming as the winds come — and playing up and down with a frolicsome, mischievous blaze, that warms, and piques, and delights us.

In the summer of 1852, I chanced to be quartered at the same hotel with him in Saratoga for a fortnight or more. He was then in his seventieth year —

but still carrying himself easily up and down upon the corridors and along the street, and through the Grove at the Spring.

I recall vividly the tremulous pride with which, in those far-off days, I was permitted to join in many of these walks. He in his dark suit — of such cut and fit, as to make one forget utterly its fashion — and remember only the figure of the quiet gentleman, looking hardly middle-aged, with head thrown slightly to one side, and an eye always alert; not a fair young face dashing past us in its drapery of muslin, but his eye drank in all its freshness and beauty with the keen appetite and the grateful admiration of a boy: not a dowager brushed us, bedizened with finery, but he fastened the apparition in my memory with some piquant remark — as the pin of an entomologist fastens a gaudy fly.

Other times there was a playful nudge of the elbow, and a curious, meaning lift of the brow to call attention to something of droll aspect — perhaps some threatened scrimmage amongst school-boys — maybe, only a passing encounter between street dogs — for he had all the quick responsiveness to canine language which belonged to the author of Rab and his Friends; and I have known him to stay his walk for five minutes together in a boyish, eager intentness upon those premonitions of a dog encounter — watching the first inquisitive sniff — the reminiscent lift of the head — then the derogatory growl — the growl apprehensive — the renewed sniff — the pauses for reflection, then the milder and discursive growls — as if either dog *could*, if he *would* — until one or the other — thinking more wisely of the matter should turn tail, and trot quietly away.

I trust I do not seem to vulgarize the occasion in bringing to view these little traits which set before us the man : as I have already said, we cannot honor him more than by recalling him in his full personality.

Over and over in his shrugs, in a twinkle of his eye, in that arching of his brow, which was curiously full of meaning, did I see, as I thought, the germ of some new chapter, such as crept into his sketch books. Did I intimate as much ?

"Ah," he would say, "that is game for youngsters : we old fellows are not nimble enough to give chase to sentiment."

He was engaged at that time upon his Life of Washington — going out, as I remember, on one of these Saratoga days — for a careful inspection of the field of Burgoyne's surrender.

I asked after the system of his note-making for history. "Ah," he said, "don't talk to me of system : I never had any : you must go to Bancroft for that: I have, it is true, my little budgets of notes — some tied one way — some another — and which when I need, I think I come upon in my pigeonholes — by a sort of instinct. That is all there is of it."

There were some two or three beautiful dark-eyed women in that summer at Saratoga, who were his special admiration, and of whose charms of feature he loved to discourse eloquently.

Those dark eyes led him back, doubtless, to the glad young days when he had known the beauties of Seville and Cordova. Indeed, there was no episode in his life of which he was more prone to talk, than of that which carried him in his Spanish studies to the delightful regions which lie south of the Guadalquiver. Granada — the Alhambra — those names made the touchstone of his most gushing and eloquent talk.

Much as he loved and well as he painted the green fields of Warwickshire, and the hedges and the ivy-clad towers, and the embowered lanes and the primroses and the hawthorn which set off the stories of Bracebridge Hall, yet I think he was never stirred by these memories so much as by the sunny valleys which lay in Andalusia, and by the tinkling fountains and rosy walls, that caught the sunshine in the palace courts of Granada.

I should say that the crowning literary enthusiasms of his life were those which grouped themselves — first about those early Dutch foregatherings amongst the Van Twillers and the Stuyvesants and the Van Tassels — and next and stronger, those others which grouped about the great Moorish captains of Granada.

In the first — that is to say his Knickerbocker studies — the historic sense was active but not dominant, and his humor in its first lusty wantonness went careering through the files of the old magnates, like a boy at play; and the memory of the play abode with him, and had its keen awakenings all through his life: there was never a year, I suspect, when the wooden leg of the doughty Peter Stuyvesant did not come clattering, spunkily, and bringing its own boisterous welcome, to his pleased recollection.

In the Spanish studies and amongst the Moors the historic sense was more dominant, the humor more in hand, and the magnificent ruins of this wrecked nation — which had brought its trail of light across Southern Europe from the far East, piqued all his sympathies, appealed to all his livelier fancies, and the splendors of court and camp lent a lustre to his pages which he greatly relished.

No English-speaking visitor can go to the Alhambra now, or henceforth ever will go thither, but the name of the author we honor to-night will come to his lip, and will lend, by some subtle magic, the master's silvery utterance to the dash of the fountains, to the soughing of the winds, to the chanting of the birds, who sing in the ruinous courts of the Alhambra.

But I keep you too long:— And yet I have said no word yet of that quality in him, which will, I think, most of all, make Centenary like this follow upon Centenary.

'Tis the kindness in him: 'tis the simple goodheartedness of the man.

Did he ever wrong a neighbor? Did he ever say an unkind thing of you, or me, or any one? Can you cull me a sneer, that has hate in it, anywhere in his books? Can you tell me of a thrust of either words, or silence, which has malignity in it?

Fashions of books may change — do change: a studious realism may put in disorder the quaint dressing of his thought: an elegant philosophy of indifference may pluck out the bowels from his books.

But — the fashion of his heart and of his abiding good-will toward men will last — will last while the hills last.

And when you [1] and I, sir, and all of us are beyond the reach of centennial calls, I think that old Anthony Van Corlear's trumpet will still boom along the banks of the Hudson, heralding a man and a master, who to exquisite graces of speech added purity of life, and to the most buoyant and playful of humors, added a love for all mankind.

---

[1] Chief Justice Davis presided over the assemblage, and brought to his duties a dignity, a sympathy, and a quiet humor which went far to make the occasion memorable.

II.

TITIAN AND HIS TIMES.

TITIAN AND HIS TIMES.

Read before the Art-School, Yale College.

I AM to speak of that great painter Titian — of the times in which he lived, and of the influences under which he wrought. Born in the year 1477, he did not die until the year 1576 — lacking only one of a completed century.

Within the limits of that century, outlined by the Life of Titian, Columbus found his way to the end of his voyagings Westward, and Vasco de Gama closed his great voyages Eastward; Luther was born and fought his fight, and died; and so did Calvin and Melancthon.

The reign of Charles V. of Spain, of Francis I. of France, of Henry VIII. of England, all began years after Titian was born, and all ended years before Titian was dead.

The same is true of those kings of Art — Raphael and Correggio. Bramante, the first architect of St. Peter's, and Michael Angelo his successor, were both his contemporaries.

Lorenzo de Medicis had hardly begun his splendid domination of the Florentines at the birth of Titian, and the career of his more famous son, Leo the Tenth was all to make, and all to end, fifty years before Titian died. He survived fourteen successive popes, and fourteen successive Doges of Venice. In his boyhood the foundations of Henry the Seventh's Chapel were laid at Westminster, and he lived to hear of Queen Elizabeth become one of the great monarchs of Europe, and of her favorite, Sir Walter Raleigh, plotting voyages for colonizing Virginia. Within this stretch of years Loyola arose and founded his great society. The Inquisition was established; the Moors were driven out forever from the halls of the Alhambra. The Eastern seas and Adriatic were swept by Venetian and Turkish fleets — coming by turns to grief. Over and over the tide of war surged through the length and breadth of Italy — sometimes wrenching important Venetian cities on the mainland from their allegiance, and again drifting them back to the always eager clutch of the Queen of the Adriatic.

These battles, however, these reigns, these great

names of which I have made mention only as a sort of index to the great and brilliant period over which Titian's life extended, will have little concern for us to-day — save as they may now and then throw a little effective cross-light upon the subject of Titian's Life, and his surroundings.

His native place was a little mountain town, Piave di Cadore. One may pass through it who goes by the Ampezzo Valley from Southern Bavaria to the head of the Adriatic. It was dependent on Venice in the fifteenth century — lying southward of the higher ranges of the Frioul, which made the natural boundary of the German region to the north. There are mountain torrents there — gorges — jagged peaks — tall dolomite cliffs and shaggy remnants of forest: — in his day an old castle of Cadore crowned one of the lesser heights. There is not much that is pastoral, save here and there a ledge where goats and cattle browse; — very little to win or keep regard, except of a lover of the picturesque.

The village lay some sixty miles from Venice, almost due north, and from the tallest of the neighboring heights — on clear days — glimpses may be caught of the far away silver sheet of the lagoon with the city of the sea floating in the middle of it.

They show the cottage where Titian was born; — certainly he had known it as a boy if not born there.

His father was a man of position — with such record of good fighting days and of fighting ancestors before him as gave him rank with patricians.

How or why the young Titian made choice of the art of painting in which to work out his career, cannot be fairly told. There are apocryphal stories of his doing boyish work with the juices of crushed flowers — hard to be believed. He may have heard of Cimabue and Orcagna — still more probably of Giotto and Squarcione, who had done work in the near Paduan country; and the current stories about Giotto and his great fame through Italy, were such as might well kindle the ambition of an adventurous boy: possibly, too, he had seen some of the prints of Mantegna's engravings. However this be, it is certain that he had a strong art craving, and that his father took him as a boy (scarce turned of twelve — if so old) to Venice. His journey would lie through Conegliano and Treviso, in whose neighborhood he would begin to see stately villas of Venetian patricians; and thence, by a broad drive, amid other villas growing more and more frequent, and made gay with decorative frescoes, he would come to Mestre upon the shores of the lagoon, whence he could see the blue line of the towers and houses of the floating city. A two hours' row from this point would land him upon the piazetta of San Marco.

It was about the year 1490. Venice had indeed passed the zenith of her commercial power and rank. The conquest of Byzantium by the Turks had cut off much of her Eastern trade — notably all that through the Black Sea and countries beyond. But still there was no richer State — no prouder one. No city so full of luxury and of all delights was to be found in Europe. A king's palace in France or England would not match the home of a Foscari in Venice, in beautiful and luxurious appointments. A king's wife in the West wore no robes richer than those of a Venetian merchant's daughter.

There had been no wars in those water streets: there were no battered towers, no machicolations, no port-cullis. The green tides lapsing and swelling with scarce distinguishable rise or fall, were their pride and their defence.

No church in Italy was so gorgeous, or had such wealth of decoration as San Marco. No ambassadors to Western Courts were so instructed, so decorous, so proud, so astute — as the Venetian ambassadors. It was a grand thing to be a Venetian in those days: and the boy Titian was Venetian, and his father before him, and Cadore was Venetian: who will not believe that the boy's heart leaped with an exultant bound as he first set foot upon the Piazza of San Marco?

The Ducal palace was much what it is now — save that the tints of the marble walls, and the sculptures were fresher, and under the arcade one looked in that time sheer through to the centre of the enclosed court. The great columns of the Piazetta were in place — and the tower (saving only the belfry and loggia which are of subsequent date). The Church of San Marco was all itself — brilliant with its mosaics, and carrying the golden horses above its portal, without suffering from such blaze of color. The tower of the Horologe was not then built, but through a cleft in the houses, at the same point, stretched the Merceria gorgeous with all manner of showy stuffs — hanging from balconies — hanging athwart doors; there too were displayed saddle housings, richest Cordova leather, mosaics, Venetian glass of every hue, jewels, tresses of gold chains, mirrors, rare bits of carving in wood, in ivory, in marble — a blaze of wealth and decorative art of which our Young Visitor could never have dreamed in the wilds of Cadore. He would have seen too in comparative freshness those Byzantine palaces encrusted with various marbles now wholly crumbled and gone: he might see those others, too, of stancher build, with great medallions of porphyry and precious stones, with which Philippe de Comines was so delighted — and yet others, then in the first lovely glow of their freshness, glittering with fillets of white marble running round pointed windows, and wantoning in flamboyant whirls upon balcony fronts—of which the Foscari and Ca di Ferro are types, visible to-day.

He would be struck too by the varied costumes —Greek, Turk, Armenian—with furred robes from the Baltic. And if he encountered a great dame upon the narrow *calle*, she would very likely be followed by a Nubian slave in white cloth, while she would show robe and cap of blue, with her yellow hair bound up—may be—with a fillet of gold.

Now observe, that what would most challenge the admiration of any visitor, in looking over the bewildering and enchanting variety—of the front of St. Mark's—the splendid maze of exhibits through the Merceria—the piquant costumes of the Levant and of the North countries, and the lustrous splendor of the walls abutting upon the Grand Canal (before yet the great Renaissance palaces were built)—would be the *Coloring* rather than the *Form*. This was far truer of Venice in that day than of any Western city.

If therefore the young Titian in his early dreams of conquest in the domain of art thought first of color—as the weapon of conquest, who can wonder?

The walls, the stuffs, the very waters and sky of Venice taught him sharply this supreme lesson through every noon-day, and in every burst of morning over the Adriatic.

But what was the influence of those who at that time in Venice represented pictorial Art?

For a long period Byzantine Art had held ground there: Venice had in fact introduced Byzantine Art to the West, having herself pierced the loop-hole through which had poured those warming Levantine rays, that had waked Western Europe into life. It was natural that Venice should feel a tender regard for Byzantine traditions: she could not forget the golden birds that had warbled in the gardens by the Sea of Marmora at a time when all the music of Italy was only the scream of a falcon.

But however strong the Byzantine traditions (kept alive during the closing years of the Eastern Empire, by the presence of many cultured Greeks in the city of Venice) — strong, I say, as this may have been, it was not in human nature that men should go on forever setting up saints in pairs — each with a hand lifted equi-distant from the head, each with a tiara of jewel work, and each set up in a compartment of its own. The school of Murano, with Gentile da Fabriano, and the Vivarini had made protest against exceeding severities in their work a half century before Titian: and when he came to Venice the two brothers Bellini represented a far fuller measure of the ease and grace and life of the realism which Giotto had taught.

I suspect Titian in his apprentice-days would have looked no more admiringly upon any painting in Venice than upon that Madonna, by Giovanni Bellini, with its two little angels, and its four flanking saints, which in Titian's time showed its tender grace and loveliness in the Church of the Frari, and which shows the same grace and loveliness there to-day.

We should have looked to see Titian at once associated with such men as the Bellini: but his father may be, was a Byzantine conservative : so Titian went with Zuccato a worker in mosaics—one of the Guild of Art : and the guild included workers in leather, in jewels, in carving. Painters did not then, or for a long time afterward, look down grandly on decorators. What Titian did with Zuccato we do not know : hard work undoubtedly, and gained that comprehension of lines, and their force, which he needed. Later he is under Gentile Bellini, who must then have recently come back from Constantinople where he had been at the instance of the Sultan, and where "it is said" he had opportunity to study the shrinking of the muscles, and the disgorgement of the veins from a head cut off in his presence.

Gentile Bellini remonstrated with Titian for his free touch, and bold, dashing way — so no doubt did Giovanni Bellini, under whose direction the young artist wrought, after Gentile's death. Indeed Titian encountered no one in those young days in full sympathy with his bold, large manner, save the young Giorgione — just of his own age, but more instructed ; and through whose influence he came to have a part in frescoing the new walls of the *Fondacho dei Tedeschi*, then recently risen at the end of the Rialto bridge. What Giorgione did there, was said to be grand : what Titian did, was said to be grander : and hence a jealousy and coolness — to which artists (be it said in parenthesis) seem foreordained. Forty years ago a few remnants of the colored friezes were still upon those walls : all the rest washed out by four hundred years of storms.

Giorgione was of a make to rival Titian if he had lived : with a fine face and figure, and full of muscular energy, he yet loved lute-playing, and all that lute-playing carried with it in those days. We hear of him as going from time to time to the pretty court which the exiled Queen Cornaro (of Cyprus) had set up in the Paduan country at Asolo — a delightful place for sonneteers and lute-players! He knew too all the orgies of free-living, and of free-loving at Venice ; and with the heat and the smoke of that sort of life, poor Giorgione was stifled, and died at thirty-two.

We do not learn that Titian went out to Asolo, or that he ever painted the Queen of Cyprus from the life: paintings of her, he did make, long after her death — probably from medals, or sketches — which have been copied over and over; one of such doubtless having given suggestions to Makart for his splendid, scenic canvas shown at Philadelphia in 1876.

Titian went country-ward more for work than for fêtes (save occasional visits to his old home at Cadore). Thus we hear of him at Padua in 1511 — doing the St. Anthony frescos still to be seen; so he must have encountered there another Cornaro (though not of near kin to the Queen), Luigi Cornaro, who had a grand house in Padua, and the finest collection of paintings and bric a brac — who had lived a wild life till forty-five—then reformed, and at eighty-one told the story of his reform, and of those methods of abstinence by which he survived till past a hundred, and which made him competent to write comedies at eighty-five. His extreme limit in eating was, he says, twelve ounces of food and fourteen ounces of wine *per diem*. Perhaps Titian gained hints from him that contributed to his hale old age.

Another city he visited in those days — but only after repeated solicitations, which his growing fame made necessary — was Ferrara. The name calls up now a grim, great castle reeking with damp odors and with grass-grown streets straggling under its murky shadows. Then it was the site of a brilliant court. Alfonso I. (a remote ancestor of Victoria of England) held it — held it hardly out of the chances of war: He loved art and letters: he gave a home to Ariosto: he solicited the favors of Raphael, and Titian: yet more, — to show his resolution — he was the fifth husband of that much-married and beautiful woman Lucrezia Borgia. I do not know if the latest historic authorities count her a wholly virtuous creature, or a woman disposed to slight irregularities: but I do know that it is a great pity that we have no undoubted picture of her by Titian to throw in as a make-weight in settling the question of her guilt or her innocence. Her lip as he would have colored and turned it, and the eye as he would have set his flash of light upon it — would have helped, seems to me, largely — in determining if she connived with her bad brother Cesare and more wicked father, or set them at defiance.

To Titian's visitings at this court are due, with other good work — the famous Bacchus and Ariadne now of the National Gallery, London; a head of Ariosto — a noble head of Alfonso, and most of all, a rarer picture — long time set as a panel in the palace walls — and known wherever art is known — I mean "The Tribute Money."

It is a small picture — scarce three feet by two: little more than two heads and two hands of the Christ and Pharisee, and a bit of drapery. It is not in Titian's usual manner before or afterward : lines are clearly defined : the finish most elaborate. Albert Dürer had been lately in Venice. Albert Dürer and Giovanni Bellini hob-nobbed together : Each admired the other. Did they possibly stimulate Titian, by criticisms upon his gloss of color? Vasari says — it is miraculous — stupendous. The ringlets that fall from the head of Christ are distinct even to the dividing of one hair from another: the very web and woof of the red tunic and the blue mantle of Venetian dye — (for painters of that age were not archæologists) — can be traced to a thread. Yet with this nicety of detail there is none of the stolidity of Denner : It will bear close look : it will bear distance. Through lesser merits, the broad bold seizure of the subject tells grandly : The calm, marble-like front of the Christ, with clear cut features — benignant look — an awful dignity — makes the shrewd, keen cunning of the low, swart Pharisee — more ignoble : and the hands below repeat the contrast, and emphasize the answer, in every tint and line — "Render unto Cæsar the things that are Cæsar's."

The painting is now hanging in the gallery at

Dresden. Titian did not follow up this style of treatment: indeed he is averred to have undervalued and spoken slightingly of its method:— Not the only time that a young artist in a whirl of enthusiasm, or of caprice, has accomplished work which has scored with the noblest efforts of his maturer years.

It is of record that on these early visits to Ferrara, he with two attendants were furnished rations weekly, after this schedule:— "Salad, salt-meat, oil, chestnuts, oranges, tallow-candles, cheese, and five measures of wine."

His correspondence too with the Duke is of record — from which I quote: "I am entirely at command, should the drawings be considered unsatisfactory, and am ready to furnish others; because having given myself body and soul to your Excellence; there is no pleasure I esteem so great as to be worthy of serving when and where Your Excellence may think me fitted to do so." For myself, I do not like the tone of this: and there is much that is even more abject in letters to other princes: The truth is, he was a born courtier, cunningly seeking favor and patronage. He had a quick eye for gain, and all the avenues of gain — full of Venetian sharpness in his bargains, yet making great gifts to princes who were sure to repay him roundly. He had manœuvred so as to possess himself of a sort of brokerage at the *Fondacho dei Tedeschi* — very like one of our custom-house appointments — with a snug salary attaching, and little to do : He had also put in claim in these times for work upon the Ducal Palace — thereby making soreness of feeling between himself and Bellini, who for a long period had governed matters as he chose upon the Piazza of San Marco.

He is invited too, by his old acquaintance Pietro Bembo, who now holds high position under Leo X. to come to Rome and plant himself there. What if he had : and measured forces with Raphael and Michel Angelo ? But he did not : Navagero — another friend, who with Aldus Manutius had founded the Aldine Academy — advised Titian to remain : Bellini was getting old, and place would soon open for him. Only Pordenone and Palma Vecchio could be called rivals : the first chiefly in fresco, and Palma in the tender and winning delicacy he put into the faces and hands of his saints.

Titian was now forty : unmarried still ; — living at a house midway between the Rialto and St. Mark's — working hard — notably in this time upon that great canvas of the Assumption of the Virgin for the church of the Frari.

Every one knows it — from gazing on it at the

Belle Arti, where it now hangs, or from the engraving of Schiavone.

The twelve stalwart apostles filling all the foreground — above them the great rift of intensely blue sky — then the billows of cloud held up by angels on which the Virgin stands with light feet, lifting her hands and rapt face to the opening heavens where the Holy Father is girt about with disporting cherubs.

The Frati — for whom it was painted — were disappointed at first — would have declined it perhaps, except that the ambassador of the newly elevated Charles V. — then upon the spot, offered to take it off their hands. Perhaps the friars missed in it that effluence of sanctity which would quicken slumbering devotion to the Holy Virgin. Indeed Titian did not paint divine faces even at his best: He is human through and through. His saints and angels are magnificent creatures; but we feel that the same blood is flowing through them as through us. There is no trick of attenuation, or dimness, or phantasmal splendor to cheat the mind, and make mystery. He does not make strong appeal to those qualities out of which religious sentiment is evolved: his saints, however well-looking, do not breed faith in saintship. He is as incredulous of the supernatural as the Agnostics of our day. He cannot bring it within the limits of his conception. He has always his intention well in hand: he dominates it thoroughly: he grasps its every side — a complete, undoubted, intellectual mastery — into which any vague beatific range of sentiment has not entered. Holy Virgins as many as you like: blood and tissue and veins all perfect: but the secret of their charms under his brush must lie in their humanity, and not in an intangible somewhat (which some great painters have seemed to reach) — a somewhat, subtler and finer and diviner. Titian's brain worked on the honest level of his eyes, and not above them : but those great eyes saw miracles of light and life and color, where you and I would have seen — only a neighbor's face!

When, or why, or where, Titian married I cannot surely find: but at forty-five or thereabout, he was living with a wife Cecilia, who became the mother of that renegade son Pomponio — for whom the father secured ecclesiastical preferment, and who went through life dishonoring his father's name, and his priest-robe, with his deviltries. Orazio was another and better son who worked with the father, and died shortly after him : there was a daughter Lavinia too, known by many pictures of her which the father loved to paint—a good example being that of the Berlin Museum — a buxom lass in brocade dress, holding up a dish of fruit and flowers, her head half turned backward, and her face full of innocence, and archness, and bloom.

But Titian was not eminently domestic — at least not in our sense of the term. He loved beautiful things outside his own doors — sometimes, it is to be feared, to the neglect of those within them. Venice invited outsidedness. Lanterns lighted up the Piazetta and the arches of the newly built palace of the Procuratori (which flanks St. Mark's Square to the south) and the Merceria, long before such luxury was known in the barbarian cities of Paris and London. The gondolas were always inviting: so was the beautiful house and garden of Navagero upon the island of Murano: the little Aldine Club made up of Navagero, and Trifone Gabriele, and Ramusio — the scholar and traveller—may have drawn him at times to its sessions: for he was a noted talker — *parlatore bellissimo* — says Mutinelli, and was a friend of these learned ones, who, in company with Aldus, had given that great reputation for accuracy to the editions of the Aldine classics.

But Titian was in no sense literary: he never grew into intimacy with Bembo — who was nothing, if not a man of letters. He loved good talk — but not Latin, nor Greek. At Ferrara, he had never taken to Ariosto: nor had Ariosto taken to him.

Yet there was one literary friendship which Titian formed, that was so extraordinary for its object — so extraordinary too for its constancy and its duration that I shall take a few moments to describe to you this man who became twin-fellow of Titian for some thirty-five of the best years of the great Artist's life. This was Pietro Aretino, or as he called himself upon the medals which he himself caused to be struck — the Divine Aretino. His humor was very great, his cleverness remarkable, his learning most moderate, his impudence amazing, his conscience—nowhere.

He came to Venice in 1527 — came there because it was unsafe for him to stay in Rome ; unsafe too, to stay in almost any other considerable city of Italy. In some quarters he had made himself obnoxious by his obscenities — in others by his blasphemies, in others by his fierce lampoons. He was eminently presentable — a master of all the outside courtesies of life. He wrote satires so witty and ingenious that all clever people wanted to read them ; and so ribald, and scathing, that all the victims wanted to kill him. It sheds a lurid light upon the smaller courts of Italy in that day to find that such a man had the intimacy of nearly all its princes. He wormed himself deftly to the bottom of their little state secrets, and made merchandise of them. Personal weaknesses, or vices he detected with the quick instincts of a beast of prey, and played with them in his dainty piquant verses, as a cat plays with a mouse. I have sometimes fancied a likeness between this polite ruffian, and the newspaper interviewer of our own day.

But withal, he had some humane qualities: he was generous with his ill-gotten, but abundant means. He really loved some people and befriended them to the last, though poor, and incapable of the slightest return. Many a poor damsel was dotted with his moneys; many a poor lad fed freely at his house. He loved luxury, and his home was luxurious: he had a keen eye for good work in Art, and his walls shone with gems of this sort. Many a prince was indebted to him for a clever thing by Palma, or Giorgione, or Bellini. He brought to Venice strong letters to the Doge Gritti, and was well received. The Venetian historians rather plume themselves upon the fact that the Lion of St. Mark gave protection to such men: it is to be feared that his nudities of literature were not offensive there: it is certain that the Doge made use of him in pressing investigations regarding the political status of the different Courts of Italy. He could write charming wheedling letters: it is supposed he wrote many which bear Titian's name: He was more apt than

even the Artist at flattery. He wrote letters to
Titian's boys (in after days) which might have been
by a New England deacon. Indeed, he sometimes
crazily thought himself good, and crazily thought
others shared the belief. When Titian went by order to visit Charles V.—at Augsburg, twenty-five
years later, he took a letter from the Divine Aretino,
recommending himself (Aretino) as candidate for
place of Cardinal, and begging that his august
Majesty would use his influence in his behalf with
the Pope. I suspect his Majesty when he read the
letter, let fall his great nether lip with a droop of
wonderment.

Of course Titian painted Aretino — perhaps many
times : We know one, which gives him a fine face —
aquiline nose — large, open eye — round forehead,
fringed with thick, curly hair. In point of fact this
fine face was seamed with sword cuts, and bore
scars from bludgeons, before Aretino reached fullness of age. How came about this strange friendship?

Titian may well have been drawn toward one who
had such appreciation of his work : Aretino again
was in the way of finding new patrons, and stimu-
lating the admiration of old ones : the open-handed
living of the poet — would have had its fascination
for Titian — so would his graces of speech and man-

ner: and I suspect, his looseness of conduct, and orgies, did not greatly disturb the shrewd, calculating man of the world — which Titian was. He painted many subjects at this time of coarse intention for which doubtless Aretino found eager purchasers among his old acquaintances at Rome.

But the master was doing far better things too: I need only mention that group of the Pesaro family at the Church of the Frari (still there, and which every traveller makes it a duty to visit, and where it is a delight to linger).

To this period belongs also the famous Peter Martyr of San Giovanni, in which—if it be true of any one picture—his power found culmination. He competed for this work with Pordenone and Palma, and distanced both. It was not in the usual manner of an altar picture. As you approached it, three or four great trees with sparse boughs shaking in the wind caught the eye: then — one of Titian's own skies, with scuds of cloud drifting over it: a dim distant landscape in the lower left corner — perhaps the loved peaks of Cadore: in the boughs of the trees were two cherubs with palms; on the ground below, the prostrate martyr with eyes and hand uplifted— the murderer gathering his forces for the last fell stroke: and the attendant in a craven panic making off — with his robes dashed about by the wind.

There was not much sanctity in it, but a strange power: the cherubs did not cheat one into a wish for martyrdom, but there was a blending of the pomp and splendor of nature with the awful possibilities and passion of human life that made one pause. Thousands have been spell-bound by this painting, who have no conception of its technical merits.

The picture—burned, with the church in 1867—was finished in 1530: in 1529 Michel Angelo had been in Venice, flying from Florence where he had been taking part in the last, sad, vain fight, for the liberties of that city. Doubtless he met Titian: and there are touches upon the torso of the murderer of Peter Martyr, and in the swarthy muscles of his arms, that look like Michel Angelo. As Titian had signalized the visit of Albert Dürer by the painstaking nicety of the "Tribute Money," did he not possibly wish now to show his power to do things as Michel Angelo had done them?

Those two great artists could have hardly grown into sympathy, and did not—now—or later on at Rome. Titian was essentially a courtier and a man of the world, ennobled by his great passion for painting. Michel Angelo disdained the pomps and pride of life, finding compensation in his ecstatic devotion to all forms of Art. Titian, at a hint from Aretino might very possibly be painting a loud bit of Heathenism for some lascivious-thoughted Cardinal, while Michel Angelo was whetting his sword for a thwack at the last of the tyrant Medicis in Florence: Titian's ear would tingle delightedly at sound of the jewelled spurs with which Charles V. and his great array of Spanish grandees came clinking into Italy in 1530; while Michel Angelo would have ground his heel in the dust, and scowled defiance. Titian could easily forget — if he had ever cared therefor — that under the rush of the squadrons, of this great monarch — whose power was felt from the Netherlands to Naples, and from Poland to Gibraltar — the last flickering blaze of independence for the little states of Italy had gone out: he could forget that the princes of Italy — patricians of Venice among them — swarmed ingloriously about his court when he came to Bologna to be crowned. But Michel Angelo could not forget these things, nor fail in his work — of speech, or poem, or marble, — to show signs of a bitterness, by reason of them, that was sublimed by genius.

Titian first painted Charles V. at Bologna in 1532 — after that monarch's return from Vienna. Titian had indeed gone to Bologna — through the devices of Aretino — on the monarch's previous visit, but it was to paint a fine woman of Bologna who had enslaved one of the chief officials of Charles' Court: It was thought—by Aretino, by Gonzaga of Mantua, and I dare say by the Seigneury of Venice — that it would be a clever thing to conciliate this high officer of Charles' Court by a portrait from the hand of Titian of the Italian dame who had enslaved him.

Yet it is due to Titian to say — that he did not come into Charles' favor by such an uncourtier-like procedure. Charles loved painting almost as much as he loved power; he had seen Titian's work at Mantua and had expressed a wish for a portrait from his hand.

That painting is now in Madrid: He is represented in a gorgeous costume— a black cap with a white plume — a silken dress — a white mantle of stiff brocade — sleeves of striped stuff— hose slashed and striped: the right hand plays with a dagger, the left is fondling the head of a gigantic Spanish hound. The eyes are blue and steely: the beard and moustache red, and the protruding lip is there which still marks the inheritors of his blood.

The monarch was charmed by Titian — not less by the splendor of his work than by his grave, courtly obsequience. Titian understood this nice sort of flattery.

He received imperial payment — which the Artist shrewdly invested in lands about Treviso; honors were showered on him, and he returned to Venice Count Palatine — his children ranking as nobles, and he as Knight of the Empire entitled to wear the golden spur and the sword and the chain of the rank.

Of course Aretino would prepare a fête for him on his return, in which also Sansovino the architect — another great friend of the two would have joined : perhaps also the learned Ramusio, now become an ambassador, and Sanuto the historian. It was a grand thing to be signalled for distinction by the monarch of whom even the Seigneury of Venice stood in awe. But the home of Titian was not what it had been : his wife was dead : he had gone from San Samuele to the north shore where now stretch the *fondamente nuove*—but where in that day the waves of the Lagoon plashed upon open beach and shore. A great garden stretched from his house to the water's edge ; and from his balcony he could look across his garden parterres, upon Murano belching fires from its glass-works, and upon the towers of Torcello, and to the left see the blue hills of Cenedo piling in the distance, behind which lay his old home of Cadore. There he passes the remaining forty odd years of his life—save some few journeys of which we shall take note ; always at work—always calm—always triumphing. Lavinia his daughter is growing up under his eye, and the boy Orazio is learning from the master the handling of the master's brush. Pomponio, the priest son, is drifting— always sure to turn up when great payments have come in. Aretino berates him for squandering his father's money.

Titian laments to his physician that he has humors of invincible idleness: but the working faculty on his good days must have been prodigious: more than a thousand pictures throughout Europe are now catalogued as Titian's, while hundreds have probably been lost. The continued patronage of Charles V. put an enormous value upon his pictures: only those with princely purses could compete with such a monarch; and Titian like a good Venetian never worked below the market price. To be painted by him was to be put upon the roll of distinction.

His method of painting did not change materially with years — save that his touch grew bolder and freer, and his colors less varied: and this — not from the haste or indifference which are apt to attend years, and established reputation — so much as from the wide knowledge, and conscious power, which had come with his vast experience.

Aretino boasts in a letter to Paul Manutius that Titian could throw off a likeness as quickly as another could scratch the ornament on a chest. This facility and the enormous prices he commanded from individual patrons, led to the neglect of larger pictures which had been commanded by the Seigneury. In 1537 the Council of Ten made order, that whereas Titian had been given a broker's patent in 1516 — yielding one hundred and twenty ducats a year, on condition that he should paint a canvas of a land-fight on the side of the Hall of the Great Council, looking upon the Grand Canal, and since that time had drawn his salary without performing his promise — that such state of things should cease, and all the salary received be refunded.

This brought Titian to task; and the famous battle of Cadore was painted — which with all others in the Council Chamber was consumed in 1577. Vasari, who visited Venice shortly after, and who was the guest of Titian as well as of Aretino—(through whose agency indeed he came,) declares it to have been the finest picture ever shown upon the walls of the Ducal palace. The Council of Ten at the same period assigned to Pordenone, (the only conspicuous rival of Titian at this date) the decoration of other apartments in the Ducal palace,—work which would naturally have fallen to the great painter, had he kept fairly by his engagements. A feud grew out

of this between the two rivals which came near to
blood-letting; nor can any one doubt that the stern
Council of Ten took a pride in thus demonstrating
that they were not over-awed by the world-wide
reputation of the great Artist.

But Titian was not beholden to them for task-
work. Charles V. endeavored to entice him to
Spain: Urbino would have given him range of a
palace: he was offered the place under the Papal
government which had been filled by a brother
Venetian, Sebastiano del Piombo.

All these he declined: but we find him journeying
to Rome in 1545, — his first and only visit. He took
Urbino in his way, and the Duke equipped him with
a magnificent convoy, so that he journeyed like a
prince. His son Orazio is with him, and both are
received cordially by the Pope, Paul III., and by
Titian's old acquaintance Bembo — now a cardinal.
Bembo says Titian is full of wonder at the antiques:
and he himself says in a letter to Aretino, 'I wish I
had come to Rome twenty years ago': and yet, with
those antiques earlier in his eye, is it not possible
that he would have withdrawn, in favor of line work,
much of that power which was lavished upon color?

He meets Michel Angelo again: but we hear of
no warmth in the meeting. He paints industri-
ously while in Rome, leaving with other work that

wonderful picture of the Pope, his grandson Ottavio, and the Cardinal Farnese — now in the Museum at Naples.

Returning to Venice, and to the suppers with Aretino and Sansovino, he had hardly settled in his old avocations before he is summoned by the Emperor Charles V. to Augsburg: and he sets off, an old man of seventy, to traverse the mountains of the Frioul in the depth of winter: but the Emperor with lavish hand has provided money and attendants: he is received with the old honors, and paints there the great picture of Charles in armor, and mounted, as he rode into the field at Muhlbach.

He has hardly returned to the honors and greetings that once more awaited him at Venice, when he is summoned anew to Augsburg — this time to meet Philip, who has come from Spain to ingratiate himself with the German people (a vain task) and whom Titian paints in such flattering way — notwithstanding his narrow chest, his spare legs, his eyelids like rolls of flesh, and his projecting under jaw, as to captivate Mary Tudor, our Bloody Mary of England, who was his betrothed bride. She was enamored of the portrait — more enamored than either she, or any other, was ever enamored of the man.

But Titian found his account in the flattery. Melancthon, who happened in Augsburg at about that date, speaks — perhaps with a touch of jealousy — of the distinguished attentions shown to a great artist of Venice. Wonderful old man — whom neither the court ceremonies, nor the great canvases on which he wrought, nor the fatigues of mountain travel in winter can break down! The next August he is again at his easel in his garden home — twenty odd more years of distinguished work before him which we cannot trace: twenty more years of sharp outlook for neglected pensions, and royal moneys which are due, but not paid: his courtliest letters all having some little touch of the trader — grown not less shrewd with age : now it is a misunderstanding as to the price their "Excellencies" have made — again it is a draft on which he has heavy discount to pay, and begs their Excellencies kindly to remit, etc.

All the while the charming suppers. "I found Aretino there," says a visitor, "who repeated sonnets for our delectation, and Nardi the historian : and viands and wines were of the finest: the discourse gay, and at midnight we looked out upon the water, where were floating hundreds of gondolas adorned with beautiful women, and the air full of charming music."

But Aretino's hold on life was not so strong as the painter's: he died as he had lived — at a supper which held over until three of the morning, and the immediate occasion was over-laughter at some unseemly joke. Titian lamented him more than the world has: yet under all his bestialities, and his fopperies, there did lie a small — a very small core of goodness which the artist found and felt.

Vasari visits Titian again, and finds him indefatigable at his work — surrounded by beautiful objects in his beautiful home — his old friend Sansovino by him — both past the nineties, and the architect struggling to appear as young as the painter. Three years after, Sansovino dropped away, and a new sense of want must have fallen upon the heart of Titian.

But the beloved Venice over which his affections have brooded for three-quarters of a century is around him in all its beauty. Whatever falling off there may have been in the rank of Venice as a state — politically or commercially — the splendor of the city was undimmed. If the older exterior frescos were fading, and the marble incrustations chipping away from the elder Byzantine palaces — the new Renaissance structures of Sansovino and Lombardi were in the glitter of their first freshness. If Famagosta had fallen and Cyprus slipped into the keeping of the Turk, the three great gonfalons were still streaming as proudly as ever over the Square of St. Mark's.

In no mart of Europe could the traveller find such rare, and costly, and accurate editions of Hebrew books, or of the classics: no where such gorgeous stuffs — such wealth of inlaid armor — such show of delicate gold work, such curious and tastefully carven furniture.

In no great city was such quietude, such municipal order, such sense and evidence of full security to person or property. Palace doors were flung wide open to the water: the stranger could look through their delicately carven portals, sheer across the marble halls into gardens where Oleanders bloomed, and from which came at noon-tide the drowsy hum of the locust.

More than ever the grip of the Oligarchy was knit firmly upon power. Into the hands of the twelve hundred patricians who every Sunday at three (by the tower of the Orologio), met in the Council Chamber, all rights of the people had passed long ago, as steadily, as tranquilly, and as surely — as day passes into night.

There seems to have been something in the very quietude of this stately company of patricians which captivated the imagination of the sailors of the streets. It was never boisterous, wordy, asserting itself. Noise of angry debate rarely came through the great windows of the Council Chamber. The gondoliers and Stradiote soldiers lounging upon the quay under the Palace, might hear the click of the balls which the noble voters dropped into the urns; but rarely, voices. Its most terrible edicts came in whispers. Its arrests were the quietest imaginable: a billet countersigned — an armed attendant to show the way. It was a subdued and elegant company — never forgetting itself to hasté — courtly, impenetrable, jealous of kings — doubly jealous of the Pope, yielding nothing to either except on direst compulsion.

In Titian's great painting of the Presentation in the Temple, there is a group of long-robed figures looking with kindly condescension upon the Virgin as she goes up the Temple steps which admirably represents the dignity, the cool courtesy, the conscious power of the Venetian Patrician.

On fête days and under cover of the mask, these men may have had their unbendings. Those were days in which Venetian jollity ran riot. There were comedies enacted in the courts of palaces (no theatres as yet); there were Bergamesque singers trolling out quaint rhymes at street corners, charlatans, learned monkeys, Egyptian jugglers, and great ladies with faces blinded in point lace picking their way through the throngs. Padua and Treviso sent hordes of their well-to-do idlers to these fêtes: and travellers from the lampless narrow streets of Paris, and from sooty, foggy London, contrived their journeys so as to be present at the great festivals of this floating city. It was a distinction in those far-off places to tell of having passed the season of a carnival in Venice:—a still grander distinction if the traveller could boast of having exchanged compliments with the distinguished Veronica — a poetess of that day (whose poems were printed at the Aldine Press) beautiful — who had been the guest of princes, who gave charming entertainments — the most brilliant type of a class of Aspasia-like women of that time who were not unread in the classics, specially Catullus and Ovid, and who fed upon the sonnets of Aretino.

But I think if you and I had been at such a fête, in such a time, we would have looked out more eagerly for the passing of the old man Titian — perhaps attended by his daughter Lavinia: we should have known him, I am sure, by the respectful way with which the crowd would have opened for his passage — and by his tall figure and dignified presence, and long, white, snowy beard, and tunic trimmed with fur, and black velvet cap, and great, keen eyes flashing from their sunken orbits.

Upon the visits of great princes to Venice, there were, of course, fêtes of exceptional importance. All the arts of the city were represented — sometimes upon the Square, sometimes upon a great range of galleys which passed along the Grand Canal — the Murano galley all mirrors and crystals; the masts and decks of that belonging to the Jewellers Company flashing with emeralds and pearls; and the armorer's ship, covered with every imaginable weapon, polished till they shone like silver.

These royal fêtes indeed of that commercial republic prefigured our present World's Fairs: it was a blazon not made only for show, but with a shrewd eye to the development of trade.

The last of these in which Titian could have participated was that given in honor of Henry III. of France, who stopped at Venice on his way from Poland to his new kingdom, in 1574.

The beautiful Foscari Palace (for himself) and three or four adjoining palaces for his attendants were put at his command. The Bucintoro — the great barge of State — bore him to his quarters, and transported him to the great banquet in his honor at the Ducal Palace. The Venetian chroniclers roll down page on page of pretty superlatives in describing the splendor of the show, with which they sought to impress him with the wealth, and taste, and skill of the Republic.

Of all this — we note only that the young king paid a personal visit to the home of Titian. And we can imagine how the courtly old gentleman would have rallied his last powers to give fitting reception to the young monarch — of the fourth generation in descent from that Louis XI., who in Titian's boyhood was living at Plessis, and hanging upon the trees of his park those who provoked his anger.

The next year the plague came to Venice — not raging fiercely, but making coy approaches. Perhaps this, perhaps his ninety-eight years suggested to Titian the provision of some burial-place. So he bargains with the Franciscans of the Church of the Frari — to paint a picture for them — a Pietá — to go against cost of burial in one of their chapels. And the old man of ninety-eight enters upon his task. Sansovino is not there to cheer, to suggest, nor Aretino to criticise, to admire. It is a virgin, with the limp, dead figure of Christ in her arms. We may suppose that a vision of Lavinia — long gone out of his household — of Cecilia, still longer gone — of Violante, a memory of his young days — may have flitted on his mind as he traced the last womanly face he was to paint.

He finishes the picture: but true to his old trading instinct makes trouble about terms, and the canvas does not pass to the Frari at all.

The next year brings the plague more grievously. But what should *he* fear in the plague, who has outlived a century of battles, who has seen fourteen doges slip from their places and die — who has seen other seasons of pestilence when the dead lay rotting on the banks of the *Rio*.

At last, however, it does overtake him — alone — in that fine house of his looking out toward Murano. Many of his choicest pictures are around him — rare sketches by his friends — books of sonnets by Aretino — bits of sculpture; models given by his old friend Sansovino, Byzantine trinkets — charming Murano wine-flasks — the chain and the golden spur of his knightship. But the pains give him grip — then come the swellings under the armpits — the constriction of the heart, and the end.

There are chroniclers who say his house was plundered before Titian died: but it is not to be believed. Most victims of the plague, by State order, were hurried to the Lido shores for burial: but in the great artist's case exception is made, and with pompous official ceremonial — the body is borne to the Frari, where he wished to lie.

It is a huge ungainly church in its exterior — flanked by a great mass of conventual buildings. It does not lie on the Grand Canal, but is only approachable by the little Rio of the Frari, or by tortuous paths leading from the Rialto. An irregular open square, upon which tall houses notch at various angles is about it. Its walls dingy, weather-stained, and showing no trace of art save in the delicate sculpture about the frieze, and around windows and portals, and the little turrets at its angles.

Within, it is cavernous, gloomy, massive. There, is the pyramid tomb of Canova, with its guardian angels; there is the famous monument to the Doge Pesaro held up by four gigantic Moorish slaves in black and white stone; there too, near by, is the well-known Pesaro picture by Titian — and in the sacristy, that canvas of Bellini's to which I have alluded as being the one which would have most charmed Titian, of all that were in Venice when he came there eighty-five years before. But the stranger will look with most eagerness in the cavernous recesses of that damp old church of the Frari, for that glittering pile of fresh marble (erected by the Austrian Government) under which rests the body of Titian — the greatest master of color whom the world has known.

NOTE.—The elaborate work of *Crowe* and *Cavalcaselle* supplies all material facts respecting the life and work of Titian, while the local coloring in the foregoing paper, is derived largely from *Mutinelli* (*Annali Urbani*) — from *Sansovino* (*Città Nobilissima*) and *Gallicœiolli* (*Memorie Venete*).

III.

PROCESSION OF THE MONTHS.

PROCESSION OF THE MONTHS.

Among the Snows.

THE book of all other books which makes us count our time, and change our dates, and reckon the seasons, — I mean the Almanac, — gives us flight into the country. Who cares when the moon quarters in the city, or when the sun rises, or when the tide falls? We want open fields to get good sight of an eclipse; a comet is but half a comet seen from a city sidewalk. The reading of court calendars, and prices current, and election records, carries us straightway into the atmosphere of towns, and calls up the close smells of conventions and of exchanges; but a record of the seasons, and a calendar of the months, measured, as they are, by the uprising and the down-setting of the sun and of the moon, somehow makes us yearn country-ward. Such record demands an horizon; and what horizon is possible to a man pitted under the slanting roofs of a city? The sound of the marching of the years is heard never so distinctly as when we have an ear upon the turf. It is hardly possible to call the roll of the months, without calling the roll of the fruits and of the roses. The old almanac-makers did well in wedding their pages with ruralities, — flinging an arabesque of flowers over the tale of the spring and of the summer, and bordering their winter calendar with the wonderful snowy cornices which the winds fashion along the edges of the hills.

All the pretty legends of soft winters in the tropics, and of oranges in January, — however true they may be on the warm bights of the Florida shores, or by Pontchartrain, — will never make us forego that old association of snow and rime and icicles with winter. Even the English ruralists, whose practical knowledge of snow-storms is limited to the feathery wonders of a day, cannot abjure the grand sights which roofs laden with snow will throw into their pictures of winter. The Mistletoe and the Holly of the holiday poets are never so green, and never so glowing with crimson, as when they shine against a background of wintry white. I suppose that Thomson (of "The Seasons"), being a Scotchman, may have seen a good many sharp flurries of snow, and possibly may have assisted at the digging out of buried flocks on a winter's morning, after a great night of storm, under some lee of the Cheviot hills; but it is certain that the story of such work is to most English readers of the poet only a snowy legend.

Still more apocryphal, apparently, is the frosty selvage with which Horace, again and again, edges his songs or odes; but though we think of Italy as a land of summer and sunshine, these descriptive dashes of the poet who rusticated amid the Sabine hills, are true to the occasional wintry phenomena of that region to-day. The Albanian hills have their exceptional cloakings of white, and Soracte does sometimes lift over the horizon "like a snow-heap."

Farther to the northward, but still under Italian skies, experiences are often more Arctic. I can recall vividly a day some thirty years gone, when the deep snows over all the flat lands which lie about Padua so encumbered the roads that no diligence would venture out. What a dull January day it was, to be sure! The peasants slumping in through the freezing slough; the long-horned cattle treading with curious reluctance through the strange white mire; the thinly clad street people rubbing their hands with true Italian significance, and declaring it "a miracle, — *sicuro!*" The weak blaze in the yawning fireplace, whipping out great clouds of smoke; the great roof of the great hall of Padua streaming with the unaccustomed drip; the marble palace of the Café Pedrocchi all a-steam with soaked feet, — I would have given the best book in my luggage for a fresh reading about Shylock and Portia that day; but there was no Shakespeare in the market.

Amid all the discomfort, however, of such January weather, the peasants wore pleased and hopeful faces, and quoted their proverb, *Multa neve, multa pane*, — "Much snow, much bread." If the benefit arising from the infrequent and fleeting snows of Italy can have given rise to this proverb of the South, how much more reason have we of Northern latitudes to bless such a tender protection of the grain roots. Nor is it protection of the grain only; many a May day we rejoice in some extraordinary luxuriance of lawn grass or of pasturage, attributing it all to a season of abundant rains, when I think more than half of the overplus might be safely credited to that persistent covering of snow which through the preceding winter kept the grass roots warm, and gave an accumulated vigor to support the growth of the summer. The chemists tell us, moreover, (if I do not mistake,) that snow-water carries with it a larger proportion of ammonia than an equal weight of rain, by which it would seem that these feathery white clouds of snow sweep down from the atmosphere a great amount of available nitrogen which would else be lost; and it is certain that what gifts they do bring in this way they keep nestling close to the little rootlets which so crave it, and so riot under supply.

Let no man then sneer at the snow. It kills only where rash adventurers intrude upon its storehouses, — as on the slopes of the Swiss mountains, or the heights of Colorado. It warms and cherishes and fertilizes (in its quiet way) we know not how many acres of grain land and sward land. Its crystals are all jewels, so rare that the handling wastes them; its bulk so vast as to make the sources of rivers; its tint so pure that the artists despair of it; its fall so gentle that the grass bends not, and yet is buried. Let me commend as a topic for a country clergyman in winter, that text from Job, "*Hast thou entered into the treasures of the snow?*"

There is an old artistic tradition which puts the month of January in the guise of a young babe (typical of the New Year), making a bold front of it, and not — like Shakespeare's babe —

"Mewing, and — "

disporting, to the great discomfort of the nurse. For my own part I can never think of January as a babe, whether methodical in its habits, or the contrary; but rather as a fine old gentleman with frosted beard, who has seen his best days, and is content to take his ease by his own chimney-corner. And if I were to symbolize February, it should be as a decorous, white-haired, venerable lady, — something shorter than January, — who is not over-clamorous for rights, but yet has her storms, and who, like many another venerable lady is most effective when most serene; as for March, she should be some shrew of a maid, following up the old people with a tremendous clatter of brooms and great clouds of dust.

Everybody supposes that these three opening months of the year are hard ones to struggle with in the country (where the almanacs, as I have said, always invite us). But let us test the matter in the most prosaic way in the world, — by actual summing up of their chills and cares and opportunities.

Paterfamilias, bestirring himself at sunrise, scratches a hole through the frost-work upon the window, and looks out. There is a world of snow upon the lawn, and upon the fir-boughs, and upon the rooflets of every gateway and arbor; even the twigs of the maples carry their narrow burden, and the rosy light of the new-risen sun puts the whole scene a-glow. No thought obtrudes of delayed and over-crowded horse-cars, of weary tramp over neglected sidewalks. Already the pet Alderney has broken her path to the spring in the meadow, and the twin calves are snuffing and pawing at the strange spectacle of the snow. The doves are alight upon the stones at the edge of the fountain, and are cooing and billing in the low-slanted sunlight, as if the whole white covering of ground and tree were only a bridal decoration. Upon some bit of snow-highroad, gleaming through under the loaded trees, there is a long trail of oxen, coiling down the hills; a half-dozen stalwart neighbors, each with his team and his goad, are breaking the path and breaking the silence with a muffled murmur of speech and laughter. Pat, too, near by, is shovelling briskly at the footways, and a lorn sparrow or two, catching sight of the welcome gravel, come twittering to their old forage ground.

There is a gay clamor of young voices, and a half-distinguishable odor of steaming dishes, as if breakfast were nigh; not a strong odor, but just enough to carry a little flavor of hospitality in it, and a quickening of the morning appetite. This latter is sharpened too, very likely, by the slightest possible chillness of the chamber atmosphere. I could never fancy those country houses where the temperature above and below is kept up to full city figures, so that a hot sameness is round the occupant, into whatever room he may wander. A little smack of frostiness in the air, that puts a healthy tingle in a man's nose and cheeks before toilet is done, seems to me a very capital appetizer, and a great preparative for enjoyment of the keen blaze that shall presently greet the master, flashing out over hearth and rug and faces.

I love to think of our country gentleman marching up to his fireside of a winter's morning, and chafing his hands — almost in the blaze, as if it were a Heaven's blessing. I can't think of his entertaining any such gratitude for a patent steam-heater, that has kept his blood in a sort of tropical lethargy all the night and all the morning. Of course such labor-saving, underground contrivances will be adopted; but why work them up to the city scale of the seventies and the eighties? Why not keep them to the honest, healthful range of a good Mayday morning, — in such sort that the children may carry roses in their cheeks, and the blaze of a breakfast fire be counted a god-send?

A practical word I want to drop here, in regard to those wood fires; you think they must be of seasoned hickory, or that all counts for nothing. It is a grand mistake. If your wood be of oak, or basswood, or soft maple, or of apple-tree (for old orchards are coming down in these days), by all means have it well seasoned. But if of hickory, or black-birch, or white-ash, or rock-maple, you may get as cheery a flame out of the green wood as out of the dry, and will besides enjoy something of the aroma of its freshness. I speak of the fire, of course, after it is fairly ablaze. The kindling process must have proper kindling material.

The winter's breakfast in the country being done, what then? I naturally suppose there may be another fire sputtering and flashing on some library hearth, whereat a quiet pipe is not absolutely tabooed; and I am certain that the blaze and the broad-mouthed chimney will together whisk away the wreaths of smoke as fast as they are formed.

The morning paper is necessarily a thing foregone; it may be eleven, under the snowy time of the year, before the day's budget of news shall be opened; but what shall we say to a page or two out of some convenient and manageable and dainty volume of Pickwick, — bringing to the hearth the hospitalities of Dingley Dell, and the tender humanities of the stout man in gaiters? Or what if it be some one among the many "Friends in Council;" or a bit of the dainty gossip of "Elia?" Will not these possibly be as good aids to digestion — whether of breakfast, or of any moral purpose suffering entertainment, as any morning paper of them all?

Then what good, square, quiet working-hours affront one in the country, with breakfast (and pipe) done, and the sun streaming into the south windows, and the fire leaping on the hearth! Or if no hard work is in hand, 't is only a longer "Grace before Meat" with Chas. Lamb; a little lingering at the round table of Sir Arthur Helps; a fingering of the freshly-cut magazines, and tender conversation with the flowers that are blossoming in the window. The bulbs must have their water changed; the mosses a fresh sprinkling; and some radiant purple Cyclamen must have its dead bloom plucked away.

Or, there is some pet Alderney to be visited, who is near her time; or some bevy of Southdowns; or, a tramp in high water-proof boots to some corner of the wood-land, where a clearing is to be made, and where a half-hour's swing of a cleverly hung axe will set all the blood astir, and more than equal a draught of the best bitters upon the market.

A little later, Jack, a stout cob, is harnessed to the "cutter," and one may whisk away to town — not one of the metropolitan centers, maybe; but in the days of telegraphing who cares for centers? The budget of letters and of papers, with which the dinner-table is presently overspread, makes home the center. All the news comes without its jostling and its uproar. Even the worst stories, by reason of intervening space and time, will be winnowed of their harshness and foulness; the master may read of political schemings with the same trustfulness with which better-informed men would read of schemes of benevolence.

If there be letters, there is abundant time for reply; two hours or more for work, in door or out, if hard work is in hand; abundant time too, before candle-lighting, for a new drive to the town, in which certain little ones — their school-hours being over — can put new roses in their cheeks, and laugh away the frostiness of the winter's twilight. Between firelight and lamp-light, the country twilight vanishes, and the winter night begins.

"Long?"

Yes, long; three, four, five hours, with (maybe) no visitor from without.

"Dull?"

As you count dulness; but with a good book and a good blaze at one's side, it would seem easy to keep dulness under; even if there be dulness in the book in hand, the fire-light makes one a kindly critic. The slightest touches of humor grow broad, and dimple out into great pools of mirthfulness, if the reader can but keep his feet warm at a good blaze.

Then there are books which seem to belong to the season of evening firesides in winter; which take their best coloring under such a glow, and the big-hearted men and women of their pages step with old-time courtesies out of their wordy enthralment, and sit with us in the fire-light.

Shall I name these, and turn my screed into a catalogue?

It is better that each reader should find them for himself, — the books that make him the kindlier, that give image and fulness to his humanities of speech or action; old books, many of them, of which he first stole the reading under cover of the lid of his school-room desk; books he hid under his pillow at night; books whose story twined with his dreams.

The Holidays too—hardly gone past—have left behind them their sweet old flavors of nursery legend: some new and tenderly touched picturing of it, has brought out once more the plaintive old ballad of the Babes in the Wood; or Cinderella has come in golden state, — why should she not, who by patient and uncomplaining toil has commanded friends and power? Doesn't Little Red-riding Hood, bring back every winter-time, in her ruddy cheeks, and under her scarlet mantle, a good wholesome odor of the English booklets, which in our young days came from St. Paul's Church-yard (Mr. Newberry's, on the corner)? And has not the Wolf — if we can only keep him outside the door — a piquant holiday air? Shall we pack dear old Mother Goose into limbo, because she gives utterance to an idle, jingling fanfaronade once a year? Do we not listen gravely, week after week, to others of her tribe — in editors' chairs and elsewhere — who cannot bring the rhythmical resonance of the nursery to aid their preachments?

And here is old Robin Hood again and his merry men all — lithe and brisk and debonair as ever, in the wondrous fine pictures which Mr. Pyle has made of them, and which make the little people of our parish wish that "Ivanhoe" should be pulled from its place upon the shelf, and the story of the Clerk of Copmanhurst and his buffeting match with Richard the Lion-hearted, be read over again. And what shall be said, pray, of "Eton Montem" or of "Lazy Lawrence?"

Or, maybe, the mechanic of the little crew is plotting a new hutch for the rabbits, which are reported to be outgrowing utterly the old quarters. To-morrow there will be a plan for another dove-cote, where a new couplet of the fantails is under report, since yesterday.

What if small jokelets run round the board (it is a generous table where our young folks are grouped): Who has given away that first-blooming primrose in the window, and to whom? Who lost their locket at that last sleigh-drive, and who found it? Up to a certain point the little creatures, Mag and Jim and Harry, will take the jokelets kindly, with a just perceptible tinge of red (not from the fire-light) running over their fair faces; but if the matter be pressed uncannily or stoutly, there comes a crimson shadow, and a shiver, and likely enough, a great fresh burst of tears.

Well, well, 't is to be hoped no more grievous tears will ever come, — only a May shower, that Mayflowers will be sure to follow.

Possibly — though staid neighbors might shake their heads — there is a little side-table drawn out, and four oldish ones, grouping themselves thereat by a kind of free-masonry, set their wits to a good oldfashioned rubber of whist, — not so sharply played as "good Mrs. Sarah Battle (now with God)" might have urged; but with a decent silence and quietude.

——Not so dull after all; and a half-moon, shining full upon the snow, cannot decoy to a drive to town. Nine — ten — eleven by the clock; the little ones all drifted away; the last rubber ended; the hearth all white and red; the moon still shining on the snow; to-morrow, the bulbs which have been making roots in the dark must be potted, and the Beurre d'Anjou grafts looked after, and Daisy's calf. A half-hour before midnight, and the frost we brushed away from the window-pane in the morning is all alive again, shot and reshot in marvellous white crystals. My lady's lace in the city is not prettier; my lady's lace in the city is not purer!

There are storms in February, — fierce, mad, driving storms; let them patter and beat and roar; the fresh-cleft hickory or birch, all aflame, will roar them back again. I think a man never feels his proprietorship of house or home more bravely or more boastfully than when, with a good fire leaping on his hearth, he looks out upon roads all turned to rivers, and the sky covered with a maze of dripping and pouring gray.

But St. Swithin (whatever may be his dim history) yields at last to St. Valentine, most rollicksome and piquant of saints. Have we watched the stationery latterly to see what wonderful arabesque borders have grown upon the note-paper? Have any pair of little fingers been practising upon doves a-cooing?

Of course it is all very absurd, as Miss Propriety will tell us with the greatest earnestness; but then, you know, Miss Propriety has no such wealth of golden curls — no such young, fresh blood, which will have its little bounds and spring-tides and ebbings. The doves will coo, though all the proper buzzards in the world were to go flapping over. We do not, of course, mean to say that a madrigal is better than a sermon, or that a Valentine should come once a week; or that, amid the great shower of white missives that go packed in the burdened mail-bags at this season, many saucy and wanton things may not be said; but saucy and wanton things are said every day by those brutally inclined. The ravenous kites are always swimming in the air for a dash at the sparrows; but none the less the sparrows twitter in pairs.

Shall we count it very great harm if some generous lad, not yet out of his "roundabout," puts a bright conceit of his own into words of tender admiration, and with a pressed flower, or border of Cupid's artillery, and ribbons to match, consigns all coyly to the Mail — he counting the hours with nervous apprehension, until the carrier shall have delivered the missive to some fair Viola? Any harm if she, on her part, welcomes the tender tribute with a pit-pat of her little heart, and guards it sacredly for a whole week — which is about the average life-time of Valentine sentiment?

It is, after all, only a little advance spray and flying jet of the great storm of sentiment which will, later and once for all, overtake them both. Vaporous now, and not very harmful, and consigned without a pang to the humdrum postman. But when, in the years that are approaching, our lad becomes on such errand his own letter-bearer, and carries his name and heart in his hand, let him invoke St. Valentine for a choice of one worthy and good and true and womanly, so that neither a week nor a month shall end the sentiment, but his hearth and home evermore be brightened, as if the years were all one great Valentine Day.

So — we cannot find it in our hearts to abuse St. Valentine ; a weak saint, no doubt, but kindly disposed, and with a smack of mirth in his saintship. We lift our hat to him, and turn to our cucumber pits.

Whoever wishes good cucumbers in the early spring must see to their planting in February. The Early Frame or Russian, I should say, for variety ; and let no one be misled by the books into trusting to the heat of an exhausted salad pit. I have yet to learn of a crop, whether of field or forcing house, which will do its best in the trail of another crop, without fresh treatment and appliances. Least of all is a good crisp cucumber an exception.

The ordinary salads for Easter day should be coming forward now, — chiefest among them that rare one, the French *Romaine* a congener of the Coss lettuces which we know by the British catalogues ; but more delicate and varied than they.

The Parisian gardeners (without the *Banlieue*) count some fifteen varieties; and well grown and well bleached, an adroit person can break the leaves of either by a tap of the finger. It is a pleasure to *fatigue* such a salad in March; its crispness is a last reminder of the icicles.

Before we know it, the bees are out, languid in the sunny weather, — such sunny weather as the harridan March vouchsafes, — about the clustering purple blossoms of the Mezereon, the first floral venturer of the year. It is a pretty shrub, and cherished by reason of its earliness; but its poisonous berries must be plucked away betimes, lest they tempt the little ones by their brilliant color.

Following fast upon the purple of the Mezereon, if not actually in advance of it, come the woolly tufts of the wild swamp-willow, — whose downy bud is more graceful and winning than its blossom. And then — six soft sunny days only intervening — there is a rush over the door-step, and a hurried tale that a blushing Hepatica has come to light in the corner of the wood. Even before the remnant of the snows is wholly gone, this little tender messenger of the flower world peeps from the woodland. It is greeted with a loud and ringing huzza, and the huzza is a signal to pull down the flag of Winter, and run up to the mast-head the little pennant of Spring.

Spring-tide.

IF March be likened to a shrewish and vixenish maid-of-all-work, with hair flying and dusty gown, I think we may call April an uneasy young fellow, of fitful humors, who has traditionally a far better reputation than he deserves. He cannot be depended on in any Northern latitudes; if he smiles to-day, he will be sulky to-morrow, and storm the day after. Yet — of such weight is a good reputation — his coming is always looked forward to with eagerness, and he is greeted with a heartier welcome than his fitfulness should warrant.

I say nothing against him as he first sets foot upon our Southern capes, treading with flower-muffled step through the woods, and painting green lines over all the cultivated lands. Even the dreary apologies for lawns which our Southern neighbors of the Gulf boast of, wear a verdant look at his coming, and it is only when he saunters northward, changing his coronet of gay blossoms for a scant bouquet, that he turns gay deceiver, and belies his sunniest promises with snow and rain. We would not give him so much as complimentary mention, save that he always leads in that pretty coquettish sister of his, May, and that far lovelier cousin, Miss June.

May has her frowns indeed, as every coquette should; but with what tenderness she shakes them off! Beguiling, bewitching, promising roses (but scarce ever giving them),— most lovable until the riper June comes, and with a glory of green, and blushes of real roses, makes herself mistress of our hearts and of the season.

We ring down the curtain (after the manner of the stage tactician) upon this grouping of a triad of months, and, stepping before the foot-lights, will deliver our little talk, — something wayward, yet something practical, — about these three fore-runners of the summer.

April sometimes sulks — as I have said; and whatever dappling sunshine may play about his days, his evenings are chilly, and the old fires of winter must be lighted again. Indeed those fires of April nights seem always to me to carry a more rollicking cheer in them than the steadier blazes of midwinter. With their coronal of flame they crown the long battle with the cold; even so, the good swordsman, after vanquishing his foe, will give a last exultant twirl to his blade before he slips it in the scabbard.

But that round of April weeks in which "fires at night" are still joyous and needful, is broken upon — from time to time — by days of serene and prophetic mildness — when robins suddenly appear — when blue-birds explore their last year nesting-places, and when, from the pond at the foot of the lawn, there rises in the soft, lengthening twilight the 'koax! koax!' of a batrachian choir, into which some veteran frog squat upon his haunches in a shallow of the pool, pours, with portentous gravity, his raucous and thundering bass. Yet withal there is no denying that to one used to the civilization of cities, there are many disagreeables about the country in spring-time.

First of all, the pavements are limited, or should be; and there is a sloppiness about that inevitable season between frost and thaw which does not invite to out-of-door walking. The gravel paths, however judiciously made, will carry somewhat of the general ooze and flux that belong to the refining processes of an April sun; the garden parterres are worse; and our lady friend, wandering thither to look upon the budding hyacinths and crocuses, may very possibly sink slipper-deep in unctuous mud.

The lawn and tennis-ground, besides being soberly brown of hue, and streaked in sheltered places with muddy-looking remnants of old snows, are spongy and poachy and springy, — unlike as possible to a summer's turf or to a city pavement. If the pedestrian take to the country high-road, he is no better off; nay, so grossly mismanaged are these thoroughfares in most country towns, that he will be in danger — between frost and thaw — of fairly bogging himself in the April mire. A clean boot is not indeed a great desideratum in the country; but a good firm foothold upon Mother Earth is; and I know of few walking-bouts so elaborately fatiguing as those which compel a tedious lifting of the feet, one by one, out of a sucking vortex of spring mud. Sufferers in this way ought, at once and everywhere, to make themselves the missionaries and teachers of more civilized processes in respect to country road-making, by which the low parts should have complete drainage, and all have coating of coarse gravel. The underlaying, too, of private paths with coarse rubbish and cobble-stones — without which security against spring upheaval and dampness, no permanent paths should ever be made — would contribute vastly to the comfort of the walking cousins from town, as well as to the neat air of a country-place. It must be remembered, moreover, in the interests of economy, that the more thoroughly a path is underlaid with such rough draining material as I have hinted at, the more secure will it be against the encroachment of weeds. A soil made up of coarse gravel, with only enough of clay to bind it well, and lying above eighteen inches of brick-bats and cobblestones, is not an inviting one for either weeds or grass to fasten themselves strongly upon.

But however prudently and judiciously paths may be planned and constructed, there must be a season, longer or shorter, between frost and thaw, when country walks will not have the enjoyableness of a city pavement. There is enlivening occupation enough, it is true, for an enthusiastic proprietor, — the unswathing of the bandaged roses, the lifting of the raspberry canes, the combing of the strawberry beds, the coaxing of the jonquils, the pretty cares of the conservatory; but I would advise no denizen of the cities to affront spring-time in the country till the ground is fairly settled, and he finds firm footing on the lawn.

Again, Spring in the country makes no show of that quiet repose which many outside people count upon as giving greatest zest to life there. It is, on the contrary, a bustling and stirring and labor-full period; we are getting the pulleys in order, and the traps, and the scenic machinery, and there is a close smell of oil and lubricants of various sorts, and much sweating and pulling, and maybe, swearing; and some new assistants have come in, who must be painfully taught and grumbled at and discharged; and in place of lovely green, there are great fields of dirty brown, where seed and filth must lie sweltering together for months; and trees are naked, and gardens are at their worst, and biting storms with snow-flakes spotting them, drive in upon fresh-dug ground and chill the nodding jonquils; and there is no leisure for carrying out any little inviting plan of a rustic seat here, or a new path there, for the teams are busy, and the men are busy, and care and every-day oversight tasked to their uttermost. Now all this can be enjoyable to none who do not see the end from the beginning, and whose hearts are not enlisted in country work, as well as in country repose. Such know that the curtain will be lifting inch by inch, — that the trailing wood plants, and the scattered streaks of green in sunny places, and the yellow bells of the Forsythia, are promises of the glory that shall presently be opened over the whole scene.

Therefore I would say to all who do not love work in the country, as well as idleness in the country, — Stay on the pavements until the gardens are planted, and the fields green, and the apple-trees in bloom. It is true that a good disciple of Father Tull, or Cobbett, or any earnest agriculturist, florist, or simple ruralist you may name, would scorn such a staving off of the real labors of the country; and I think we can pretty safely gauge a man's really earnest intentions, rurally, by the date at which he leaves city for the fields. If not till later June, you may be quite sure that he cares as little for grafting as for planting, and that all his knowledge of fruit lies in a good appetite for ripe specimens. Such a man's advice, if he offers it upon a rural subject, is not worth the catkin of a filbert-bush.

If your citizen turns his face field-ward in May, before yet the pear-trees are in their bloom, there is more hope of him; he may come to the grafting of an apple-tree, or the proper planting of his melons. But if he confronts the mud of early April, and is in at the planting of his Early Rose (the most profitable, if not the most excellent, of all early potatoes), and the overturn of his winter composts, and the sowing of his Early Bassanos or Egyptian Beets, there is hope that he has good weaning from the pap of city luxuries.

But because a man shows this promptitude and urgence, it is by no means certain that he will keep up what is called a fine place. A fine place, as popularly understood, grows out of system and precision and nicety and abundant funds, and can be arranged by contract, and put on show at a great lift of the roadside, like a lay figure in a haberdasher's window. But the rural zeal that braves all the awkwardnesses of earliest spring-time is not so much enchained by thought of *ad captandum* results, as by curious and loving study of *processes*.

A fine pear — nay, a very fine pear — can be bought any day in the market; but the amateur can never buy in the market the pleasure with which he watches the healing and re-incorporating process of some grafted scion of a *Beurré d'Anjou;* there is no possible appraisement of the tender and enjoyable pride with which he looks upon the first tokens of a successful knitting of graft and stock, or with which he sees the crimson cheeks coming at last upon his closeted *Bonnes de Jersey.*

Yet there are abundant amateurs who having satisfied their special inquiry (by minute observation of daily development) with respect to any particular fruit, abandon or neglect the culture; not from lack of rural appetite, but only because their attention is directed to some new inquiry. Having conquered one fact, they leave it with the good people of routine, and range about the field in search of new conquests. Your gentleman of business method, on the contrary, with no new horticultural scent to divert him from the well-ordered trail of his gardener, is most exact in his labors and most nice in his accomplishment. What may be the quality of his secret gratification at the bestowal of some horticultural premium, it would hardly become us to inquire. I think it will be found that the most zealous ruralists are rarely the holders of showplaces; they are too earnest in search of special facts to give their mind to those harmonious combinations which come within the province of the gardener, and which command popular admiration. The best and most zealous pharmaceutist is very apt to show but a flimsy array of drugs, and his shop is aptest of all to have the air of a laboratory, rather than the attractive glitter which belongs to the establishment of a popular apothecary. A good gardener, like a good apothecary's clerk, will keep the property of his employer in most excellent order, whether the master or proprietor be an enthusiast in the matter or no.

I have hinted that spring-time in the country, with those who are given over to rural duties, brings bustle and haste and seeming confusion. It is altogether the poorest time in the year to design cautiously, or to carry out carefully any schemes of improvement. Every open day, when once the ground is fairly settled, must be given to the plough. The fences which winter storms have slanted or flung awry must be made straight and sound. The beleaguered water-courses, whether on newly seeded fields or in old meadows, must be cleared. The young clover must be rolled, and if the land be light, a rolling will do no harm to the winter grain and to the fresh-springing oats. But amidst all the rolling, and the ploughing, and the heavier and less-welcome preparatives for crops to come, let no man who has a home in the country forget or overlook the tree-planting of spring.

Why not in autumn? Surely in autumn; but if a man does his best in that more leisurely season, there will be always something left for spring; it will be all the better, indeed, if the pits have been prepared over winter, and the old turfs with which such holes should be dressed shall have been ripening for plant food, under the snows and frosts. Of all the composts in the world for giving leafy vigor to a newly planted fruit-tree or shrub, I know nothing better than the thoroughly decomposed turf from the borders of an old grass field. The evergreens will take kindly to the same dressing; and except you secure immediate and lusty growth to a young evergreen the season after planting, it will in all likelihood have an up-hill time of it for years. Later May is, above all others (in this latitude), the season for evergreen planting. All of the fir and pine family hang out too heavy a burden of leaves for safe struggle against the winds of winter, and only in the most protected situations can the autumn planting of any of the evergreen family be ventured upon with hope of successful results. Let me further hint, that any man possessed of a country place, though it be only of three or four acres of ground, should have his nursery bed for young evergreens, from which he may select—at will, and with an eye to form and habit of growth,—such specimens as may be thrown in upon corners, upon knolls, upon the flank of a tangled bit of shrubbery, and by one bold dash of dark green color give emphasis to the tamest bit of foliage.

It may be observed, moreover, that with proper precaution, the transfer of evergreens may be made safely throughout the summer. In view of any such necessity, it is well to keep a few specimens in the nursery bed closely root-pruned, in order that they may have a great stock of fibrous rootlets; the pit to which transfer is proposed should have abundant stock of decayed turf, and this should be kept thoroughly wet for two or three days preceding the transfer; next, a cloudy and still time should be chosen (the wind is a great enemy to the healthfulness of exposed rootlets of any kind); last, mulching should be thorough, and a stake or two with bass matting secure against a sudden flaw of wind. By observing these conditions, it will be quite feasible to dress up a knoll, burnt brown by the suns of August, with a great bouquet of Norway or Austrian green. I like these sudden instalments of color, by which we may work out miracles of contrast as deftly and easily as a painter scores it with his brush.

More hazardous, but for that very reason more captivating, are the startling changes which may be wrought upon a small reach of landscape by dashing out (with the axe) some luxuriant and tossing plume of a locust-tree, that you have tolerated for its June odors and its magnificent wealth of green, and exposing to view some previously hidden border of summer flowers, or bit of rustic trellis with a wild tangle of the Bitter-sweet (*Celastrus Scandens*) capping it and overlaying it, and reaching out from it its wavy, woody tendrils, with such abounding affluence and such wild and winning negligence as I think few climbing plants can match.

But we are running into summer, when we should stay, for a few pages at least, amidst the bloom of spring. Is there any bloom like it? Not narrowed to glass houses, like the winter bloom, not exceptional like the summer's bloom, not hiding in secluded wood-paths like autumn bloom, but riotous and exultant, and filling the fields and covering the woods. Is there anything more beautiful in nature, in a flowery way, than an old apple-orchard, its rows so broken by age, that all traces of art-arrangement are gone, its tops so gnarled that you find in them no reminder of the pruning-knife or the saw, its gaunt limbs so mossy as to simulate the savagery of a forest, and yet all canopied with tender bloom, — not white, but white blushing into pink, and pink blushing into redness? The fruit will be poor, very likely. We are not talking Pomology just now. In fact, I think nature has shown a nice compensation in this matter; the wretched sour cider fruit has I think a richer bloom than the Northern Spies and the Gravensteins. The seedling peach that lifts its delicate carmine from a chance hedge-row makes a far prettier show of color than the fat Melocoton, whose bloom is but a tawny reddish stain. I think, too, that I have seen very showy colors upon streets and in ball-rooms, which shrewd observers do not seek after to transplant.

There is the white of the pear-orchards too, not so fairy-like and wonderful as the apple-bloom indeed, but singularly pure in color; and when it invests the prim pyramids of a dwarf-garden that sentinel you, and flank you right and left with long rows of white soldiery, it charms (or should) as much as any of the embroidered parterres of the gardeners. I have no scorn for these last, to be sure; the pansies and the daisies (red and white), and the jonquils, are full of regalement to the eyes of those who have liberty of gardens; but the pear and the apple bloom, and flowery sheets upon the meadows, bless the vision of the poorest. If even the humble dandelion involved great appliances of bottom heat, and glass fondling to bring out its golden brand, I think we should give it a praise that we now deny. Its eyelets, dropped like new-coined eagles over an acre of greensward, are not least among the floral wonders of the spring.

I hear that the newer gardeners are condemning the old purple lilac as something vulgar; well, so are green grass, and the apple-blossoms, and the blue sky, and a thousand of Heaven's gifts of springtime. When I live beyond a tender feeling for such old-fashioned favorites as the Lily of the valley and the Lilac and the Guelder rose and the Striped-grass as accompaniments of a country home, I will take to wax flowers, — feeling that nature is not equal to the supply. But a love for the common does not forbid a love for the uncommon; if I choose to cherish tenderly the old white rose, — the only Northern rival of the *Lamarque*, — though its period of bloom is so short, it no way unfits me for a hearty welcome of the gorgeous red face of the *General Jacqueminot*, or for a coquettish dalliance with the pretty *Madame Louise Carrique*.

I cannot close the spring talk without some honorable mention of the fruits and vegetables of spring.

You have them better in the cities?

Doubtful. First, that little crisp, scarlet, round-bellied fellow, — the Olive-shaped radish (the most tender and delicate of all his tribe); he, at least, is impatient of long journeys after he is plucked out of the brown mould of the forcing-bed. His crispness bleeds away fast by contact with the air; and when once the wilt of long exposure has come upon him, the marketers can never build it up with sprinkling or cold water *douches*. But pulled at sunrise, for a breakfast at seven, on an April morning, with judiciously broiled chops, and feathery rolls to flank them, and the little scarlet radishes are a very grateful reminder of the garden.

Still less will the salads proper permit of package in barrels, and overturnings on market floors, and the crude handling of raw market-boys; a good head of lettuce must carry all its delicate fibre unimpaired to the table, — most of all that best of lettuces, the White Coss (the French dub it *Romaine Blonde*), which must be deftly tied up with bass matting five or six days before its true fitness comes; and then, by plucking away the outer and enwrapping leaflets, you shall reach such blanched and dewy and cool vegetable fibre as crackles under the tooth like thin plates of ice. Crown this bountifully with Bordeaux oil, a pinch of salt, the merest *soupçon* of vinegar (in which the peeling of an onion has had preliminary soak), and I think the bounties of a spring garden can do nothing more for you.

In later May comes the Early Bassano, with its delightful flavor of the earth (they bear forcing as well as cabbages, and well repay the trouble); at a quick pace, after this first garden tenant of the spring pot (I make no account of spinage and asparagus, which are legacies from autumn), there come the Dan O'Rourkes, or the Tom Thumbs, — not much to choose between them, save that the latter will involve none of the awkward labor of "bushing." The snap-bean (the dwarf China is best) tempts you awhile by the variety it affords, but gives place presently to that glory of the cabbage-tribe, and king of vegetables, — the Cauliflower. He is terribly impatient under the hot suns, even of latter May, and must be humored at times with a little artificial shade; but no product of the garden pays better for extraordinary care.

In way of garden fruits, I think none can be fairly

claimed as a spring visitor, except that prince of all, — the strawberry. It pains me to think that there are here and there, scattered about the world, individuals who, by some inscrutable providence, are unable to eat of this fruit without bodily detriment. I regard them with the same kind of pity with which I regard people who are bereft of their hearing. In latitude 40° or thereabout, the first gathering of garden strawberries dates from the 10th to the 20th of June. In a record of fifteen consecutive years, I find these the two extreme dates. Through all of latter May, especially if the season be exceptionally dry, I should advise the garden proprietor to give to his man Patrick the diversion of watering the strawberry bed two or three times a week, with a weak wash of guano; but let him see to it carefully that no blossoms are injured; I would further counsel a coy bespreading of the whole surface, with the young grass clipped from the garden terrace; and when the berries are fairly formed, I would advise him to look about the neighborhood for a good Alderney cow, in her first milk; but let no butter be made, — whatever the mistress may claim, — while strawberries last. Following these advices, and I think the most arrant citizen will find a dish, morning, noon, and night, upon the country table — between berries that are fresh and cream that is real

— which denizens of the cities pray for, and pay for in vain.

I shall not enter into a discussion of varieties. The pomologists have come to such a pass in their rivalries and jealousies, and mutual abuses, as to remind one of the virulence of the art writers, and book critics. I can only say that if I were to enjoy a good dish of old-fashioned Hovey's to my breakfast, I think I should prefer the Triomphe de Gand for dinner, and am quite sure that I should sup upon Charles Downing or the Crescent — and very likely send my Wilsons to market; (people who buy in market should not be particular). Again, if it were not a matter of dishes, but if, upon a garden stroll, I had a lively desire for a *bonne bouche,* that should be full of aroma, and require no condiment of sugar or cream, I am sure that I should pluck a goodly specimen of Lennig's White. For such wayward, stolen tastes, I know no berry that is so inviting.

What sport is there of spring time in the country? Tree planting, gardening, — these smack too much of positive labor perhaps. Tennis is for youngish blood; billiards belong to winter; boating carries one into August; the gun is hanging idle on the wall since last November. But athwart the gun there is a landing let, and a rod and a creel, dedicated to the prince of all sports; not angling in general, but that charmingest of angling, whose prey and glory is the little golden spotted swimmer, *salmo fario*.

It should be a mild afternoon of June (April will do, and so will May, and so will morning, if one can be astir at sunrise), — a mild afternoon with a gentle wind blowing up the meadow at your back, — a wind that scarce shakes the solemn tops of the hemlocks, and yet sets all the aspen-leaves astir; the brook should be fairly full with yester-night's rain, — the sun to your left, Westering fast, and throwing dense shadows of maples and hemlocks and cliff, across valley and stream; there should be such solemn quiet as to make the chirp of a garrulous and inquisitive Chickadee in the near bushes painfully distinct; and with creel half full,— a most delightful burden, — we may safely leave our spring sportsman picking his way through shaded glen, or sauntering under the stately oaks that dot the meadow, — casting his brown hackle lightly on the water over every lurking-place which he knows of old, — mindless of the lengthening shadows and of the dews, — cheated of all the village sounds that betoken eventide, by that swift music of his reel, — till at the last, far down in some narrowed ravine, the sunset and the blackness of the overhanging hemlocks bring his June day to a close.

To-morrow the summer will have come.

Old Fourth and Fruits.

I PICTURE July as a stout woman, with a liberty-cap (of '76) upon her head, and perspiring fearfully. Yet she wears a cheery, honest face and if she have none of the bridal freshness of June or May, she wears the honors of maternity, and leads in a great brood of flowers and fruits in her train. August is a dark-eyed Senorita, languishing and sighing, and with a sultry sulkiness that bursts out from time to time into clanging and thunderous storms. September is a calmer personage in the family of months, — golden-haired, I should say, with a round-moon face, and more matronly even than her sister of July — with a sickle at her girdle, and sheaves of grain for dower.

I am credibly informed that there are a large number of people who annually pass the Fourth of July in cities. They are proper subjects of commiseration for all good men. I remember, some years ago, to have been waylaid in a metropolitan hotel upon that festal day of the summer, and my regard for country quietude and my love for country seclusion have been, I think, intensified by that day's fearful experience. A great annoyance of sound can be borne; but little ones are exasperating. A roar of storm or of cannon has something pacifying in it; but the pestilent iteration of crackers and of pistols at one's elbow is maddening. I can imagine no better figure for a Tantalus than that of a pursy man perspiring in the heats of July, with a din of exploding crackers at every hand, and with no power in him to stretch out an arm, and shake the sin from the little urchins who keep up their tormenting *roulade*.

That odious metropolitan July day is remembered like a hobgoblin dream, full of whizzing sounds and cinders.

There was another Fourth, equally well remembered, and more pleasantly, when four of us, sworn comrades of travel, broke bread together, and toasted the famous anniversary in bumpers of sour Swiss wine upon the top of the Rhigi Culm, with Lake Zug lying like a mirror under the eye, and all that wondrous panorama of mountain, field, and flood simmering in a glorious sunshine.

I do not know what the habit of the boys' schools may be now-a-days: but in those old times when we wore roundabouts, and studied Adams' Latin Grammar, the Master (or "Principal," as we Scottishly called him) used to give us a day's excursion by omnibus or stage-coach on the Fourth. And we piled into and all over such vehicles, by the dozen, infesting the doors and windows and roof, — hanging about the beloved stage-coach like bees on gone-by fruit, — making the hills resound with our jollity, and waking every old farmer's barn by the wayside with the echoes of our mad mirth. The old ladies, standing akimbo in the doors, stared blank astonishment at us through their iron rimmed spectacles, and shy girls caught admiring glimpses of our spick and span new white drilling from behind the farmhouse curtains. What a triumphal progress it was, to be sure! Dew on the grass, larks singing, late roses blooming, cherries ripening, tall rye waving, the old coach crick-cracking, Tom (our wit) chaffing the driver, and the new-mown hay filling all the air with its sweet perfume. Do lads of these times know anything of such gay coaching-bouts, I wonder?

Then we stopped toward high noon at some huge, lumbering village tavern for dinner. A tavern dinner! — my mouth waters even now to think what ambrosian fare had been provided (by previous arrangement of the Principal) to cheer us boys who had been depleted with three hard months of boarding school diet. A turkey — positively a turkey (and stuffed too) — at one end of the long table, and at the other — great heavens! — a dapper, crisp, curled-tailed pig, with a sprig of parsley in his mouth, and giblets and what-not, in a little paunch-y tureen of gravy close by.

Tim Turner had never eaten roast pig; how we watched him as he slipped the tines of his fork into the first crisp morsel, and put the toothsome dainty to its crackling, final account.

"Eh, Tim, is n't it prime?"

No wine for boys in those days. I think the old master would have been mellowed by it; and very likely was, out of his private locker. But our banquet boasted a half-dozen of hop-beer, and there was enchanting music in the pop of the corks, and uproarious jollity when an over-ripe jug discharged itself full in the face of the English master, and bespattered his white waistcoat.

I wish I could hear jokes to laugh at now, as heartily as we laughed at those which went cracking up and down along that Fourth-of-July table. I think there was not a kink in the roast pig's tail but gave pleasant handle to some gibe that set the whole boy company in a roar. In short, we admired each other as persistently and loudly as if we had formed a bevy of brilliant literary men. Then we toasted the day at last, and went home through the woodlands, carrying a flag and singing songs; and there was a secreted pistol (such weapons being forbidden) which one adventurous boy loaded (he had loaded hundreds, he said), and another adventurous boy, stealing into the corner behind the wood-shed, fired it off in the shades of evening. Never one of us saw who did the firing.

Another "Fourth" of the boy times I remember being billeted upon some kind old relatives of Tim Turner, — grandparents, if my memory does not misgive me, — and there were two other boys — favored ones — who shared the invitation. A queer, cockloft old house, I recollect, and tall cherry-trees in the garden, some of them almost reaching their boughs to the chamber windows; what a wealth, too, of ox-hearts, and white-hearts, and black-hearts (names smothered now under a cloud of pomologic lore), and what havoc we made among them! Tim Turner suffering by his excess of zeal with a cruel indigestion, and a stripping, and I know not what other domestic infelicities, above stairs, at the hands of the white-haired, stately grandmamma. But cherries did n't make us sick, — not *us*. Yet I have even now crude recollections of a horrible nightmare, provoked on thought of being taken suddenly sick in a strange house, and of being subjected to the peremptory nursing orders of the stately old lady in white hair and white bed-gown.

This mention of cherries reminds me that the fruit is no longer what it was, — a fruit associated in the old days as intimately with the "Fourth" as the fire-crackers themselves, I see nowhere in excellence, save on the exhibition tables. Such luscious cherries used to hang temptingly over every dooryard fence of New England; but the trees now show cancerous black tumors, or the bark gapes open, and the life oozes away in great gummy clots. I hear of no definite and effective remedy for these ailments. And if these could be conquered, there remain the canker-worms, which over wide belts of land entirely defoliate the struggling trees; and the curculio, which, in fault of its old friend the plum, inflicts its Turkish sting, and forbids development.

I think the time is soon coming — if it be not already come — when we must look, at the East, for the old beauty of this July fruit only upon dwarfed trees which have nice garden treatment. It may be even necessary to revive the protective method of Sir Francis Carew, who, as far back as the latter part of the sixteenth century, delayed the ripening of his cherries in England, and secured a rich show of fruit by extending a gauze screen over the whole tree.

There is no doubt of the fact that, in all the old-settled portions of the country, we are meeting with more difficulties, year by year, in the raising of superior fruits. We are conquering the difficulties, to be sure, and keep the markets in fair trim; but the day when a man could stick in his sapling of a cherry, or a plum, or an apple, in good garden ground, leaving it thereafter to grow at its own will, and be confident of a full harvest when bearing-season came, is utterly gone. There must be nursing and watchfulness and pruning, and a hand-to-hand combat with a great brood of pestiferous insects.

Who that feels the gray shadows of middle age thickening over his head (for my part, I confess to it) does not remember the peach-orchard near to every old homestead of New England, and the rich burden of rareripes and free-stones and cling-stones (before yet the magnificent Melocoton was known), and how round-jacketed school-boys, with big pouches of pockets, thought it no theft to abstract a few from between the fence bars, and went their way rejoicing in spoils and perfume? Nay, there were times when we used to bring a spotted bandanna handkerchief, with the corners tied together, to the massing of such stores of peaches and blue plumbs as an old ninepence (as rare as the fruit is in our day) would buy. I think I could find my way in the night-time, even now, to the locality of an old tree that bore "June-eatings" (so the farmers called them), upon the flank of the hill that lay westward of a certain high-school; but the tree is dead, and the plunder plunderable no longer.

With the abundant and easy crops of those days, I doubt if the small school-boy thefts were ever very noticeable, economically considered. I suspect Deacon McCrea would have given us all we asked, if we had ventured the request; but then what would have become of all the romance of the rope ladder which we let down coyly from the second-story windows, after the master was asleep, and the wonderful Sindbad adventures which we had to recount?

Next after cherries, in the pleasant summer weather, came raspberries; not the modern berries, which, under pomologic manipulation, have become so dainty of stem and stalk that we must needs bury them in the winter, or lash them in straw cloaks like a *remontant* rose, but the sturdy old black and yellow caps, that lifted their thimble-like cones along many a country hedge-row. We strung them on stalks of timothy grass; I do not know if that is a child habit to-day; but three or four and thirty years ago it was in great vogue. I have a vague recollection that certain childish attentions to a blue-eyed angel in short dresses and red morocco shoes found their climacteric in the transfer of a half-score of black-caps from my spear of grass to her spear; what came of it cannot so well be recalled; but when I think of the berrying, and the July warmth, and the callous men at their mowing (it being haytime) and the red-morocco shoes, a golden mist steals over the memory and obscures the scene.

I like the good old sturdy black-cap berries, because they take care of themselves. They want no gardener's strawing and bundling. They are proof against all the insects which beset the multitude of fruits. They are rampant and vigorous and abounding. The red Antwerps and Philadelphias and Brinckle's Orange (a rarely good berry, it must be said) want petting and nursing; and ten to one, disappoint you by dying some hard winter, in the middle of their straw sheathing. But the honest black-cap is always itself, and can hold its own with the willows and alders. Not very exquisite in flavor, maybe, — not soft and spongy, but almost suffering an honest bite, — yet having a wild, forest aroma of its own, and a sure bearer.

Huckleberries come in August. I have been looking in these days of New Rochelle, and Kittatinny, and of farmers' clubs (which might as well be called advertising clubs) for a Dumptabinny, or a New Bordeaux huckleberry. Why not? Is not the little, old-fashioned shrub worth revision? Is there no fruit innocence left that can rejoice itself with huckleberries and milk? Is it a corrupt taste that covets that dish when first the summer evenings smack of the coming coolness of autumn? I am quite sure that the pomologists will have their hand (and their handbills) upon this old berry before many years are past; and I dread to think what they may make of it. Large, possibly, and juicy, and tender no doubt; but the old aroma of the wild pasture-lands, will they guard that? Can it be guarded under domestication? I have never yet eaten a tamed partridge or prairie-hen; and it appears to me that a generation or two of cage life would dissipate all the gaminess which gives now a relish to these estimable birds.

Of summer wild fruits, there remain the blue-berries, the bil-berries, the choke-berries, and a certain unnoticed little fruit (at least unnoticed by the fruit books) which in our boyish times was known by the name of Shad-berry, the product of that earliest flowering tree, which trails its white glory along the banks of our rivers and inland lakes through middle or latter May. If I put a botanical pin through this old friend, it must be with the title of *Amelanchier Canadensis.* The country people call it Shad-blow;

and the name has so far vulgarized the shrub — it will come to be a goodly tree under fair treatment — that it is hardly allowable in well-ordered collections. Yet its feathery trail of bloom — coming before all white tree-bloom of the year — is a spring messenger of peace; and if my recollections are not wrong of certain bathing-bouts to Lake Snipsic, near to Ellington, along whose borders this tree grew in profusion, the fruit is by no means to be despised. The wood of this tree has the singular peculiarity of being traversed by minute red veins; whence it came about that some of us philosophers of the jack-knives entertained a theory that it must be the Judas-tree, which thus carried all through its heart, and evermore, the signet of the bloody betrayal.

Turning gardenward in September, we meet — the grapes. But there is a war about the grapes in which we — yearly annalists of the bounties of the gardens — cannot mingle. A word must be said in praise of that vine which shows the first downy-blue clusters of the season, — the Hartford Prolific. Not over-rich in either perfume or flavor, but honestly doing its best year after year; not taking a double twelve-months' rest to recuperate; not prone to mildew or other ailments; not dropping its leaves and showing bare bunches; but a steady, homely, certain bearer, neither resenting lack of attention, nor caring for over-much pruning, but year by year showing its modest purple clusters in early September.

After this earlier vineyard show, comes first in order and in rank the little copper-colored Delaware. But, if I am not mistaken, it has not as yet at the East, an assured place in public favor. It shows a bad trick of dropping its leaves in August, leading thenceforth a pinched and asthmatic life. The berries, too, at their best and under highest culture, are not generously large; two or three together hardly make an honest freight for the tongue ; then — the flavor? Rich enough, luscious enough ; but, after all, somewhat tamely luscious, suggesting the word *cloying;* and lacking that brilliant piquancy which so emphasizes the sweetness of a perfect fruit as to make you forget its sweetness altogether.

The Iona, which takes to blushing very shortly after the Delaware, is to my notion a far better fruit, with no smothered sweetness, but great briskness and a noticeable character of its own. The bunches, too, are broad-shouldered, ponderous, and the berries are not wearisomely small, but as generous in size as the clusters. Of course, I speak of it at its best. At its worst, the vine grows haltingly, invites the thrips, drops its leaves, and shows a scant array of miniature bunches.

It is not a grape to be recommended to careless cultivators, not even to good second-rate cultivators. It demands absolutely the highest culture and extremest care. With this, and in its own zone of soil and climate (and I believe every grape has its own), it will reward magnificently. Nothing less than deep trenching and thorough drainage will serve as a preparative; if with these precautions, and deep planting, the vines sicken and grow pale, and show shrivelled leaves and weak clusters (say on the third year), exposure or soil is unsuited, and no redemption is possible. But do not make haste to condemn too broad a zone of country, because your own plants fail.

The old Concord is a steady grower, and holds rank among all out-of-door grapes, like the Baldwin among apples; not of finest flavor — never luscious, but almost always sure in bearing, and hardy as the hardiest. Westward of the Alleghanies, and on vineyard slopes that look down kindly to the rivers, this old fruit shows larger, and juicier clusters than we can boast of at the East, and a more thorough ripening to the core.

I have great respect for that old mother Concord vine, which I am told still survives in the garden just northward of Hawthorne's old "Wayside" home (at Concord). Yet it has not come to great bulk there; I have seen far larger growth, in vines of half its age.

The Diana, shy and uncertain bearer as it is, and showing the unwelcome habit of pressing its berries into unevenness of shape and premature decay, will always be a favorite for its rare keeping qualities (when thoroughly ripened) and its piquant muskiness of flavor. A noticeable thing, moreover, about this vine, is its impatience of close trimming; it does not take kindly to the "spur system;" its best crops — so far as my observation goes — come from a long, vigorous, unpruned branch of the previous year's growth; and care should be taken with the Diana, to secure these long reaches of new wood.

Then there is the veteran Catawba, about which Eastern cultivators do not now concern themselves over-much; with an early September sun pouring upon it all through October, it might make a royal grape, but save under exceptional conditions of exposure it is too slow a ripener. A score more of names might come into our list — from the delicate Lady Grape of our good friend Campbell, to the last new Hybrid; but when the last and truest praise is spoken of the best of all, it is quite certain that we have yet to look for a thoroughly good out-of-door grape — East of the Great Plains; something that shall over-ride the market, as the Golden

Chasselas tops the markets of France. The greatest drawback in quality seems to be an ugly core of rawness and sourness, which our suns do not reach or subdue. Is it possible that too fierce a heat in our sunshine (as too fierce fire under the grill of a chop-house works kindred ill effect) does somehow bring the exterior to a premature ripeness, which thereafter swathes harmfully the core of green sourness?

One word of affectionate commendation I must give to that rampant and abounding grower, the Clinton; hardly worth mentioning for its fruit, though those who recall the boy-days of frost-grape hunting will be cheated into pleasant reminiscences by its tweak of acidity and big bundle of seeds; but as an ornamental vine I bespeak favor for it, — so abounding in tendrils, so glossy in its green, so sure and firm in its foliage, so riotous in fruitage, that it is the very thing to give its thronging embraces to rustic columns, to bits of old slatternly fences, to dead trees, to staring outbuildings, to bald surfaces of wall, and to awnings of village shops.

I said September should wear a full, round face, like her harvest-moon. It should be calm, too; she represents a season of repose; all profitable growth is fairly over when her face beams its broadest, and the sun nears "the line." The grain is ripe, the roots are ripe, the fruits are ripe, the leaves are ripe, and in all their axils the germs of another spring struggle and growth are coiling into shape. No wood growth or vine growth after September comes in, is worth its cost; 't will not harden so as to bear the blight of winter. Foolish old vines and rampant trees attempt it, and show sometimes lusty green shoots or tendrils; but it is a vain show. It reminds me always of the wanton foppery of an elderly man, whose years should make him sedate; or of the vain millinery which misguided womanhood will sometimes affect, after fifty years have placed their successive seals upon forehead and figure.

The hurry of the grain-harvest is over; the mowing — even for aftermath — is over; the weed destruction, for the year, is over; but work is not over, as old Tusser, may admonish us; —

> "Thresh seed, and to fanning, September doth cry,
>   Get plow to the field, and be sowing of rye;
>   Sow timely thy white wheat, sow rye in the dust,
>   Let seed have his longing, let soil have her lust."

And so, with the jingle of this old Suffolk rhymester in our ear, and with the katykids a-chirp, and a neighborly owl lifting its *too-whoo* in the edge of the wood, and the broad moon shining, this ripe month goes out.

Seated under our bower of vine-leaves, we wave it a kindly adieu; waiting patiently and hopefully for the fairy October, which to-morrow shall kindle a new and a fiery glow over all the landscape.

Playtime, Plays, and Planting.

OCTOBER is regal, and walks the woods royally with great show of purple and crimson, while a veil of golden mist streams from the tiara of the queenliest of the months. November is a humble attendant, who wears dun-colored garments, but sports a cast-off royal veil of the queenly mistress, and walks in mists as golden as she. December has masculine chill and harshness and frosted beard, not deserving our praises save for the halo that shines round his head year after year, lighted by the wondrous Christmas star.

I believe that boys' vacations, now-a-days, come around in July, or thereabout; but five-and-thirty years ago, in those boys' schools of which I had painful experience, vacations happened somewhere in October, — possibly running a little into November, — so that the golden months, gilded by vacation, were twice golden.

We fellows, in that time, must have left our

homes in April, when as yet no leaves had shown themselves, and but here and there a stray blossom, — when the elders were looking after a planting of the peas and parsnips in fresh-dug ground, that caught a little skimming of frost over-night; but when we came back in those bright October vacations, lo! the trees were all loaded with leaves, and thick, welcome shadows slanted on paths where no shadows lay in April. What a gorgeous thing it was to take that first tramp after the return under the maples just crimsoning, under the vine-arbor all glowing with purple, through the melon-patch where the yellow-faced Cantaloupes smiled at us! We knew well enough that the Cantaloupes would not be gone; we knew some "roasting ears" would be left; we knew the Pound-sweets would be just at their best; we knew the Virgalieus — if not cracked out of all shape — would be in prime condition. And the hazel-nuts, they would be a-ripening, and the Cheeseborough russets, and possibly, *if* frost came early, shagbarks would be ready before vacation was over.

I do not know how a month could have a better naming for a boy than to be called vacation-time. There are hints now and then in the education journals and exceedingly staid newspapers about study being a great pleasure, and about good little children loving school so much that they are sorry to hear the master or the mistress say that the term is ended.

I distrust such statements very much; I think that a good, wholesome longing for vacation-time to come is one of the best possible evidences that a boy is kept up to the notch of a good daily gain. There are a great many serious things which, in our progressive days, are entertained as a joke and made sport of, but I can't help thinking that syntax and vulgar fractions and *Quousque tandem* want such a knuckling down to them from a boy as will give him capital relish for vacation, come when it may.

But while I say this, I want to enter solemn protest against the awful system of cramming which seems coming into vogue, by which a boy shall be set to half a dozen different studies at once, and his examples in arithmetic (growing to be mere conundrums in figures) shall be piled upon him twenty deep. School-book makers seem to be striving one against the other — who shall put the keenest puzzles to young brains; and school-mistresses, by the same law, assign most merit to the lad who can solve the greatest number of them in a day. Piling up numbers for the sake of numbers is a vain thing; it feeds the nervous, American unrest, which goes to the worship of cumulation. Better by odds, that a boy should go slower, with a fuller knowledge of the qualities and meanings of practical problems, than this weary floundering through the ever new subtleties of pedagogic contrivance. But I must not preach.

My impression is that we "fellows" began to score off the weeks before term-time ended fully two months in advance; then we came to scoring the days, and finally to a scoring of the lessons; and there was a certain oldish Adams' Latin Grammar drifting about the Edgewood house, a few years ago, which bore some of these score-marks upon it; and under Rule VII., or thereabout, there was a special score and an October date written in colors, with a halo of glory around it, not very artistic to be sure, but significant and impressive.

But October had another glory for the old boys of thirty-five years ago, — the school closed with dramatic exhibitions, at which Captain Absolute and Diggory (without Miss Hardcastle, it must be said) were accustomed to figure. We studied our parts in the pine-woods, we rehearsed them over the wood-shed; we borrowed wardrobe from the "hired man" and retired troopers; we dressed the hall with evergreens; we learned comic poems for declamation; we struggled hard for a drop-curtain, but the Principal decided against it, — 't was too theatrical, — so we turned a recitation-room into a dressing-room, and subscribed for extra candles, and made a night of it. What a strain and press and throng upon the benches; and what weak knees and pale faces in the recitation-room! But we brought our courage up under the bright eyes beaming on us, and the extra candles, and went through the matter bravely. There was applause — though the Principal solemnly forbade it — (quite impossible to resist Nehemiah Wilkinson, who played our head parts); there was laughter, uproarious, undisguised; somebody said that a young woman on the back benches shed tears at one part. Quite likely. I doubt if Mr. Abbey or Colonel Mapleson, with all their paraphernalia, ever kindled such relish of the dramatic art, as we, with a real pistol (the Principal loaded it and put in a thundering wad of Boston Recorder), and a militia-man's coat, altered expressly for our Captain Absolute.

No female characters were allowed upon our stage; no boy was permitted to don crinoline, or what filled the place of crinoline in those times, though we had one or two boys who would have made capital girls. So we played Sheridan without his heroine, and Goldsmith, as I said, without the Hardcastle. In fact, we had emasculated (excuse the word) editions of the plays, with no womankind in them.

But a play without a woman in it, when one thinks of the matter, is but a dull affair; virtue doesn't get its reward in it, and vice has not full exhibit; and though we kept our courage up on these short rations (dramatically speaking), there was a hankering among some of us after the real thing. As chance would have it, another schoolmaster not far away had more progressive views, and at *his* exhibitions allowed one or two of the smaller boys to personate heroines.

I remember finding my way on an October evening (I think it must have been clandestinely) to one of these exhibitions, my first participation in the *real* drama. With the master's injunctions on me, I fear there was a little guilty shamefacedness at crossing the threshold of iniquity (I mean the institution of the neighboring schoolmaster, who was really quite lamb-like in private life). But he had a green drop-curtain, and something that passed for foot-lights, and these things alone made me quake. There was a great hum and buzz and a flutter of excitement, — possibly a fiddle or two, but of this I cannot speak positively. I am quite certain there were some quite innocent-looking middle-aged ladies present; one of them tapped me with her fan and asked me to pass her "the bill." The bill — ! the bill of a dramatic performance!

At last the curtain rose,—the fiddles giving a graceful *diminuendo* to their performance—and then came silence. The curtain rose; there was a sofa,—a real sofa,—and a carpet too, for all the world as if it had been a parlor. Then the men came in,—two of Barnes's fellows (Mr. Barnes kept the school). They talked splendidly, and they sat down upon the sofa, just as any man—not playing —might have done. If I had known how rare a thing this was, I should have admired it a great deal more than I did.

In our school-house on the Exhibition nights one could see the back wall and the windows, and knew very well that the windows opened on the ball-ground and old McCrea's orchard: but at Barnes's there was a hanging behind the stage with a false door in it and a painted window, which anybody could see was not a real window; yet I kept waiting to see the false door open. At last it did open,— at what stage of the play it is impossible to tell now; indeed, all earlier portions faded in presence of the light of the beautiful Geraldine. Of course it was one of the boys; but I could not conceive of her being a boy;—such a trim-fitting pea-green silk, such jaunty little gaiter boots with pearl buttons, such a sash, such cheeks, such a voice! And she went through with all kinds of perils; and the rascal of the play would have run away with her, and I could have jumped over the foot-lights to kneel at her feet and declare myself a sworn lover (though I was of tender age for such risks). In short, the woe and pathos and pea-green silk and foot-lights subdued me utterly. This, to be sure, was real drama! All the evening I was in a tempest of feeling, — one moment assailed by jealousy, when the lover of the piece passed his arm around the waist of Geraldine, and again excited to rage almost, when the villain of the play provoked the poor, unprotected damsel to tears; (at least she put her face in her hands as if there were tears). I hoped it might be so. I wanted it all to be true. If it were only possible to console her!

At last the curtain dropped on her loveliness, and Binks (I found out his name), the odious lover, won her. I went home, — clandestinely again, — thinking of the foot-lights and Geraldine. O for a touch of that sweet little gloved hand of Geraldine! I dreamed of Geraldine. Two days after, I loitered about the Barnes brick building, eager to find some memento of that brilliant illusion, of that fairy scene, — some ring, some locket, some curl, some slate-pencil, — if that were all, — to recall the cruel past. They said it was a boy-player; but it could have been no boy. Ah, Geraldine, Geraldine!

Well, this was one of the old golden October experiences; and, curiously enough, a year or two since I happened to mention this old dramatic performance, and my infatuation with Geraldine, to a friend who had been one of Barnes's scholars. He listened kindly enough, but spoilt all by a great roaring laugh, and said he would take me that afternoon to see Geraldine. And he did; it *was* a boy. He is now butchering in Hamden; he is doing a "fair trade;" he weighs, I should say, two hundred and odd, and chews Mrs. Miller's "fine-cut." Ah, Geraldine! Geraldine! *Spem vanam sequi.*

I credited the grapes to September, the while we were dallying with that moon-faced lady, but a richer show of grapes by far belongs to October; of course a little biting of the early frosts must be looked for, but there is doubt if a twinge of cold that stiffens all the clover-leaves will injure much the flavor of a grape. The frost-grape we know is rather benefited by it; and it is by no means certain that the Isabella, if fully ripe, would not suffer a refining of flavor under a cold that ravaged the Lima beans and the peppers. To tell truth, the Isabella needs refining to make it palatable. We have sworn by it a great many years, and done sufficient honor to the Mistress Isabella (of North Carolina, I believe) to allow us now to tell the truth about it;

— to wit, that the vine is a free bearer of a grape that rarely ripens, and when ripe is only passable for eating and thoroughly execrable for wine. It makes indeed — when fully ripe — a wine full of *bouquet*, but for that very reason only fit for giving aroma to wines of better body which lack perfume. I remember seeing — thirty-five years ago — in the cellars of a Bordeaux merchant, three or four snug casks of Isabella wine — imported for the sole purpose of this diffusion of its flowery odor over a vintage of the *Graves* country. And this large exportation of American wine to France (said to be increasing year by year) is not — as many swiftly decide — for a mere change of label and easy counterfeit; but for service in limited amounts, for those courses of manipulation and the blending of flavors, and enlivening dull aromas, and mending color, and qualifying weak bodies, which belong and have long belonged to the judicious manufacture of clarets.

The fact that a grape is fragrant and grateful to the taste (in its perfect state) is, I believe, no proper evidence of its fitness for making a good wine. In respect of cider I think the same analogy holds; the Newtown Pippin makes indeed very good cider, but, if I am not greatly mistaken, the Crab makes a far better cider. The grape from which the best Medoc wine is made — such as Chateau Margaux and Lafitte — has no great reputation as a dessert fruit, and could never have in presence of the Golden Chasselas, which is without special repute for wine-making.

In this very month of October, where we linger just now, I remember having passed through Medoc in the vintage season, and recall distinctly the tameness which belonged to the grapes of the Lafitte vineyard, as compared with the luscious clusters I had eaten at Fontainebleau. And I recal, very gratefully, how the manager of the Lafitte estate took us — an old college friend being in company — into the private cellar of the Chateau, asking us to make choice of wine for the day's dinner. And there came up a dusty bottle dating as far back as the end of the last century, of which only the *bouquet* remained : It was literally — *ashes of roses*. But when we came to later cherished years, one of them among the teens, and another between twenty and thirty, there was not only delicious perfume, but a rich sound body that inspirited and cheered. If there be better wines made anywhere than on that little vineyard of Lafitte, it has never been my good fortune to taste them. The Mouton and the Latour are close by, and the Chateau Margaux less than a half-day's drive away ; but between them, singularly enough, are sandwiched vineyards which bear only ordinary reputations, and command only half-prices. We are slow in learning the lesson, in this country, which must be learned, that the quality of a wine depends upon especial exposure and soil far more than upon the species of the grape; and that a most excellent wine grape under one exposure and in one soil, may lose such excellence under other conditions — though possibly gaining in reputation as a table fruit. The taste for grape-eating is not only vastly on the increase in this country, but in Europe also. Many of the vineyards within easy reach of Paris, from which only an ordinary wine has been made (notedly those of Pouilly), are now converted into grape-orchards. And Paris has a maw for all the fruit that comes.

October and November are essentially the months for pushing forward country improvements, of whatever kind. The old race of selectmen understood this matter, (it being among the few things which came within the scope of their comprehension,) and called out the dwellers along the highways to mend the roads. And what a dreary mending it has been, and still is! Our railways stand fairly beside other railways; our machinery of all sorts is in the front rank; our inventive genius foremost; our civilization in most aspects even with that of olden nations. But in the matter of road-making, we are barbarians. You shall go away from a village shop where you can purchase the *papeterie* of Paris, and drive along a highway that would not have been tolerated by the road-masters in the time of Tiberius. We have the fastest trotters, and the lightest carriages, and the firmest skeleton wagons that were ever heard of ; and we have for their service and display the most abominable country roads that are to be found in any Christian land.

We go on shovelling the old *débris* of the ditch-ways upon the middle of a carriage track, fondly thinking that decayed leaves and old turf will make good metal for the beat of a horse's foot. There are large and thriving towns I could name, with their thirty to fifty thousand inhabitants, — with road metal all made to their hands amidst the *débris* of adjoining basaltic cliffs, — which show all through spring, and every season of wet, such sloughs of streets as are a disgrace to our century and our civilization.

I see a reason for our great slackness in this matter, in the fact that railways overtook us before any good system of road-making could be matured. If we could swim over fifty miles by steam in a couple of hours, we undervalued the difficulties that might lie upon a three-mile beat of road. The consequence is, that, in any journey before us, we think little of the hundred or two hundred miles of steam-travel, but keep a wholesome horror of the fragment of roadway which joins our railway terminus with the point of destination. The establishment of horse railways, whose managers are careful for little but their dividends, leaves the whole problem of sub-urban road-making in a still more unsettled condition.

Not only in the matter of road-making, but in all rural improvements which depend upon treatment, or upheaval of land, October and November are the golden months of the year. No earnest ruralist will let them pass unimproved. Whether grading, or clearing, or seeding, or trenching, or planting, or walling be in hand, no pair of months are equal to them in the whole calendar. The teams are in full vigor, the men are stimulated by the cool breath of autumn; there is no panting under August heat; the low marshes are in their best stage for ditching; the ground is friable and gives the best perfume to the ploughman; the nursery saplings have finished their growth, and wait for transfer; the turf has shown its most rampant growth, and will keep a velvet sleekness till snow comes.

If we come to landscape decoration, whither we must tend if we bring our civilization to its ripest form, autumn is still the time both to plot and to execute. The waning hues of the summer foliage give the best studies of color; and the dropping leaflets, as they leave bare great open spaces in the woods, open the vistas by which we may measure our plans and direct our clearings.

No better timber and no better wood is cut — for whatever purpose — than that which is felled just as the leaves are prepared to drop away from the axils of the newly-formed buds of the year to come. No hickory will crackle in the fire so merrily, and with such outgiving of its nutty aroma, as that which falls under the axe with the great *tumulus* of its ripened leaves sweeping the air in its fall. No cedar, or locust, or aromatic sassafras — for rustic decoration — will hold its bark so surely and firmly, and give such enduring satisfaction, as that which falls under the axe of later October.

In the work of tree-planting it is a mistake to suppose that we must needs wait until the leaves have absolutely fallen. It is better by far to anticipate this, and, when once full ripeness of the leafy canopy is assured, make the transfer. We thus give a fortnight or more, for good settlement of the earth about the rootlets, before freezing-time shall have come. I except, of course, in this connection, the evergreens all, whose transplanting season does not fairly come till spring. If the planting of deciduous trees must be deferred, the holes may very properly be prepared in autumn, and the turf strewn about the pits, to take the benefits of the winter's frosts. Still another item — since I am running strongly toward practicalities here — must be named for the benefit of those who have much tree-planting to do, and large transfer of trees within their own lands, to wit, — an efficient root-pruning, six months (or what is better, a full year) previous to the transfer; this will work wonders in developing the little fibrous rootlets, which most of all contribute to the support and vigor of a transplanted tree.

I had occasion to mention Shagbarks and the search for them, among boyish reminiscences; this has not yet lost its credit as a good old-fashioned American fruit, and I hope it never may. I mention it again for the sake of remarking that, by careful root-pruning six months or a year in advance, (more especially excision of its long tap-root,) it may be safely removed; and, if we may credit French experiences upon the walnut of France (very like English walnut, and a source of great revenue to many communes by reason of the nut-oil), it may be successfully grafted with the best scions of thin-shelled fruit, by choosing a young and thrifty stock of two years old, and grafting near the root, by the old cleft method, — using good bass bandaging and plenty of protecting wax. The introduction of foreign shell-fruit trees into this country, has so far as I know, not resulted in good practical results. The Spanish chestnut, and the English walnut and filbert have all been tried faithfully; and though the trees in many instances make vigorous growth, and show no apparent injury from our fierce suns or killing frosts, the fruitage is not (in any instance I have known) very promising. I have upon my own grounds a filbert bush — hardy and healthy apparently, as if growing on English soil, and maintaining good renewal of growth (by stooling) for thirty years now, yet its fruitage counts for nothing.

I look forward however to the time when a good American dinner will not be complete without its after-cloth dish of thin-shelled shagbarks, from a tree that has grown from a graft of the most approved variety.

Even into December the work of country improvements may go safely forward; the clearing of new land, the thinning of overcrowded forest growth, the planting of walls, the construction of walks and roads, — for these, severally or together, no better time can be found than that which immediately precedes the locking frosts of winter. And when the dead-lock is fairly established, — so far as treatment of the land goes, — the open, sunny weather of

December still invites us, many a day, out of doors. If we have rocks to move, they glide easily over a frosted and stiffened turf; the brambles and waste growth of outlying pastures cut easiest when the earth is locked unyieldingly about their stems; the woods, despoiled of their leaves, give free insight and outsight to their most sequestered nooks.

At last the white pall comes, which is the usher to the ceremonials that belong to the dying year. The snows may force a lock-up at home; but for us who live in the country such prospect is no way appalling; the fruit-bins are full, the wood-shed is full, and the fire-light plays regalingly over the book-shelves from dusk till within an hour of midnight.

—— And what new, strange gardening is this I see, even when the snows are piling higher against the walls, and higher along the roofs? A great green vine — such as the botanists tell us nothing about — begins to coil along all the ledges of the dining-room, and droops in wanton festoons, — now over a picture of some darling face, — now making leap across the old-time beaufet in the corner, that is all besprent with little childish gewgaws, — and now again doubling itself into a great looplet over the doorway, and encircling some wonderful assemblage of red-alder berries, that are as brilliant — saving the lack of contrasting leaflets — as any holly in her Majesty's dominions. In the window, too, within finger-long reach of the fairy crystals that are shot every morning over the panes, a tray of nodding ferns has suddenly appeared, springing from a rich mat of wood-mosses, where scarlet partridge-berries are glowing like fire; most wonderful of all, a big tree has sprung up from the floor, and almost touches the ceiling with its topmost branches, — all overhung it is, too, with a strange medley of queer-shaped fruit, which a corps of admiring young folks declare to be the best fruit they ever saw or even heard of. I am sure, too, that they think the gardening to be ever so much finer than any out-of-door gardening of the spring. And when the noon sun, pouring in, gilds all the green things, and warms the canary in his cage into a little transport of Christmas song, it makes us all forget the snows and the winds of winter.

Through all the holidays our winter garden keeps its greenness, but the fruited bonbons melt away astonishingly; and the unreasonable little gardeners have the audacity to talk of a possible fresh crop against New-Year's day. My present record, however, does not extend to that date, near as it may seem.

All that remains for me now is to close my portfolio, — to blow out the candles on the Christmas tree, — and to wish all my readers, wherever in the Calendar of the Months my message may find them — a happy Twelve-month to come.

IV.

BEGINNINGS OF AN OLD TOWN.

Norwich, 1659–1859.

BEGINNINGS OF AN OLD TOWN.

Norwich, 1659–1859.

IN the year 1859, two hundred years after the first settlement of the town of Norwich (Conn.), there came about a celebration of the event. Daniel C. Gilman, Esq., — since better known for his sagacious and wise Presidency over the Johns Hopkins University — was appointed to deliver the historical address usual on such occasions; Bishop Lee, of Delaware, another native of the town — much honored then and more honored in these latter years — was also invited to give an hour to commemorative discourse; and the Hon. John A. Rockwell — who not many years before had with high approval represented the people of that region, in Washington, was commissioned to speak about the heroism of a great captain who had illustrated the early annals of the town, by his zeal and courage; in addition to all these, the present writer was asked — in virtue of his Norwich nativity — to gather up what shreds of topic he could — after such distinguished foragers in the Centennial field, and to take upon himself a share of the speech-makings which go to swell the usual *impedimenta* of those festive occasions.

The opening for discourse, under the circumstances, did not seem large or promising; but the autumn weather was fine; long streams of jubilant people filled all the greens and high-ways of the little town; the brisk breezes of the mornings, lapsed into that sunny noon-tide stillness which put all the world into easy receptive humor; and under the huge tent — all besprent with streaming pennants — was gathered a great festive crowd, who by their cheeriness, and kindly listening repeated the outside sunniness of the air. And as I read over the periods of the Centennial speech to-day, they seem, somehow, to be so brightened and lighted up with the aureole of that time of jubilee, as to excuse this entertainment of the memories of that old town again, and this record of what I found occasion to say.

Centennial Address.

I SHALL not detain you long : indeed, after the absorption of all the salient topics of the day by the gentlemen who have already so ably addressed you, I should be at a loss to fill up even the half hour which is allotted me, did I not feel that the Occasion itself is the real speaker, and we only the interpreters ; every successive oration or poem, being only the passing of a new set of fingers over the keys of the great Centennial organ whose music is swelling and surging on our ears to-day.

And what is the occasion that has drawn together such a vast crowd of young and old, of citizens and strangers, as Norwich never welcomed before ? Only a birth-day ; or rather let me say, a great golden wedding. Two hundred years ago this month, and the masculine energy and vigor of the Puritan was married, under God, to that little mountain bride, which from the beginning lay waiting here, between the rivers and the plains. Yet what is there in the beginning of a town that should warrant such festivities? Do not all towns have their beginnings, either near by, or remote? Is it wonderful that a company of sturdy settlers, having bargained for lands hereabouts, some two centuries since, should have defended their own, and dug, and planted, and built, and worshipped, and left a posterity to dig, and plant, and build, and worship after them? Is not the story now repeating itself all over the world? Long before the days of Mason, or of Fitch, the Mohegans or the Pequots delved, and planted, and worshipped in their way, and after them other Pequots, or other Mohegans: to-day one shape of shadow which the drifting clouds of centuries cast upon the hills, and to-morrow another shape of shadow.

The mere fact of settlement is nothing; there is no distinction in being born; the question is,— what growth, what development, what fulfilment of promise? And all anniversaries have their force and their joy in this — that they are the registers of growth, and not the registers of decay. The seed you throw into the ground must germinate by a law of nature, and must stretch up a little bundle of leaves to the light and air; no thanks to you for this. But if you feed and nourish and protect, so that it comes to a great wealth of leaf and stem, and finally from a fully compacted maturity throws down showers of golden fruitage, then your pride and your joy have cause. So to-day we rejoice in the beginning of white homes on these plains and river banks, because energy and toil, and faith and courage, have assured constant and teeming growth; and the tree whose rootlets are in the dim and shadowy past — lo, on all your hills the golden fruitage!

I say that we have cause for this festive rejoicing of ours, in our growth; and yet if you do not feel to-day, looking on this sea of glad faces, or walking these streets filled with almost princely houses, that the town of Norwich has made growth enough, and set up trophies enough, and nurtured rare children enough, to make her birthday a festival, why, I shall not try to prove it to you. If you can stand in the full rays of the sun and yet deny their warmth, I am not prepared to prove that there is any warmth in them. I address myself rather to those who are hearty believers in the propriety and justice of this commemorative fête, and shall ask them to go back with me for a few moments to that old rallying date of 1659 — appearing to many, I dare say, a kind of mythical epoch — toward which on such commemorative days we strain back our imaginations, and seem to see, as it were in some mental kaleidoscope, the swart faces of savages, steel head-pieces, black coats of Puritans, tomahawks, beads, black-letter Bibles, hard work, and faith in God. But I shall not attempt to clear up this delicious confusion by any speciality of detail; I hope only to fasten on your minds, by one or two broad historic marks, the actual limitations and relations of that old date of 1659.

We weigh dates by the great facts that belong to them; and what was the rest of the world doing at the time our sturdy settlers paddled up the Mohegan river, and planted Norwich?

In the old country, of which at that time the colonists were all loving children, the truculent Oliver Cromwell had just closed his great career; Richard, the son, was too feeble to wear the mantle of such a father, and had given over the attempt. The shrewd general Monk commanded the British army, and the army held the fate of the country in its hands. There were plottings and counter plottings; Algernon Sidney and John Milton working vainly for a republic are thrust aside; the line of kings is restored; and perhaps at the very time that the Norwich settlers are marking out their home fields, crowding through alder bushes and swamps, the vain, irresolute, amiable, good-for-nothing Charles II. is journeying from Dover to London, amid all

BEGINNINGS OF AN OLD TOWN. 143

manner of rejoicing — guns and drums, and the waving of banners. In France the weak Louis XIII., who ruled by the brain of Richelieu, has gone by, and the great Louis Quatorze has just come upon the stage ; still under the tutelage of Cardinal Mazarin, but yet he has fairly inaugurated that great reign, which is to carry France to the highest splendor, through the extremest lusts of civilization. But in justice to France it must not be forgotten that while our Puritan settlers were building their first meeting-house upon the green, men of French birth and lineage, such as Le Moyne and Mesnard, were toiling through the silent forests of the West, far as the shores of Michigan, carrying knowledge of the Christian faith, and exploring and mapping out the resources of the continent. Poor Spain, which in times past had sent over the ocean a Columbus and Pizarro and Ponce de Leon, and which had illustrated our colonial annals the century before by that barbaric and daring march of De Soto through the everglades of Florida, far as the Mississippi — the golden crosses and the iron spear-heads clashing together in the cane-brakes — which had founded the oldest town on our Atlantic border, St. Augustine — was now being disabused of her golden dreams ; she was wearied by long wars with France and England, in the course of which she had lost her island of Jamaica, and was feeling the approaches of that insidious decay which is feeding upon her still. The little Netherlands, near to Dover and to the French coast, had grown bravely from that beginning of independence wrought out by William the Silent, a century before, and was now almost a match for England on the sea. It was the day of the Tromps, and the Ruyters, and the De Witts; and the Dutch flag was flying on Batavia and Java in the East, and from the heights of Good Hope, and from that little promontory of land which we now call the Battery of New York; indeed, there were Dutch houses at this time in New Amsterdam, built by Dutch artisans and defended by Dutch valor, which would rival the best houses of the Massachusetts Colony. As for the two states, with which, as colonists, we were to be brought more immediately in contact, (I speak of France and England,) I do not know how I can better epitomize and illustrate their respective stages of civilization at the date of 1659, than by saying that just at the time when the first psalms of thanksgiving were rising in the first Norwich church, the great dramatist of France, Molière, was wandering through the Provinces, playing his own comedies to crowded and delighted houses. And across the channel, the great British poet, John Milton — quite another style of man — was living in a back street of London, and sitting in his doorway, clad in a sober suit of gray — the very type and image of puritan simplicity, and of puritan faith — was turning his sightless eyes to Heaven, and revolving, in the recesses of his mind, those solemn thoughts and that splendid imagery, which in due course of time were to be embroidered — as it were by angel fingers — upon that noblest of Christian poems, the immortal epic, Paradise Lost.

Meantime there is growing up between the Yantic and Shetucket, the material for a homelier epic. Sixty, seventy, and eighty days only bring news of what is happening across the water; and it matters little to our sturdy colonists if Charles II. or if Richard Cromwell is wearing the purple, if only goodman Elderkin has built his mill according to contract, and the town surveyors keep the cart path in good order, from the Cove below, along the plain to the meeting-house above, and to the store. The clergyman is giving good, honest doctrine; Uncas, below upon the river, is a good friend, and keeps a sharp look out for intruders. The swamps are yielding gradually to cultivation. The worshipful Mr. Winthrop has secured a charter from the king, which gives all needed independence, and with slip-shod indulgence, extends the boundaries of the Connecticut colony from the Narragansett river to the shores of the Pacific — rather too liberal to be lasting, but forming the basis of that claim which in after years secured to the State its admirable school fund. And the same worshipful Mr. Winthrop, being Governor, is occasionally waited upon by the active men of our little township — Deacon Simon Huntington, or Lieutenant Thomas Leffingwell, or perhaps the grand Major Mason, who report progress to the Governor, and listen to his after-dinner discourses about my Lord Clarendon, or Sir Isaac Newton, or John Milton, or the Hon. Robert Boyle, all of whom he has personally known, and with some of whom he still corresponds.

The quieter men at home, who do not dine with the Governor, are laying out new highways, or pushing a little trade down the river and along the coasts. There are no savage onslaughts; the worst enemies the town knows, for a long succession of years, are a short crop, or an occasional wolf, or a rattlesnake, or some drunken friend of an Indian, or some new clergyman who does not hold precisely the right views in regard to the Saybrook platform. Bating these little diversions, life seems almost Arcadian here, as we look back upon it. The cattle are feeding and lowing in the new pasture grounds; the red blush of the English fruit trees is beginning to show itself in all the gardens; the virgin meadows along the Yantic are filled with flowers that perfume the air; the brooks, fuller and more numerous before the forests are cut off, frolic down all the hill sides; and of a Sabbath morning, while the dew is still sparkling on the grass and on the tree tops, the church bell from the rocky height yonder — tone after tone — tone after tone — spends its musical gushes of sound over the roof of the farthest settler.

Thus a hundred years or more pass on; the king Philip battles, and the long stretch of the old French and Indian war, bring their train of mourners; but Haverhill, and Deerfield, and Fort Edward are very far away from the homes of Norwich; as far on the score of news as Pike's Peak or the California trail are now. The growth of the town is not seriously interrupted. The original settlers have multiplied; new people have come in from year to year by vote. Death has, indeed, drawn a little array of recruits to one side, but courage and faith and work and hope are still the masters of the situation. And in this hundred years or more there have been changes in England. Sidney and Milton (whom we saw sitting on his door-step) have both gone long ago to their reward. Charles II., and Clarendon, and Buckingham, and Nell Gwynne and the rest are sleeping a long sleep in the pages of the biographical dictionaries. It is the time of the Georges and of the elder Pitt, and of that dogmatic Dr. Johnson, who thought the king could screw down the colonies by as many taxes as he chose, and of a greater man than Dr. Johnson — I mean Edmund Burke — who thought the king could *not* screw down the colonies just as he chose. Over in France, the reign of Louis XIV. is ended, and the king that the courtiers fancied too grand to die, is as dead as any pauper in a Norwich grave. There has come after him a weaker and a worse king, Louis XV., who is ruling jointly with the madame Pompadour, while Voltaire, with his sardonic smile and his witty flings at Providence and simple faith, is not only a writer, but a power in France; and he is leading on very swiftly with the rhythmical cadence of his artful and sonorous periods toward the bloody gulf of revolution. In the scientific coteries of Paris there is just now an American name well known — that of Benjamin Franklin. And there are other names well known at home, such as Israel Putnam, and Patrick Henry; and this latter has made a speech before the burgesses of Virginia which has found echo in every valley of New England. There is living, too, somewhere in his neighborhood a tall, quiet, sedate country gentleman, looking after his estates just now, whose name is colonel George Washington, and who, not very well known as yet to Norwich people, will presently make himself known and make himself felt all through the country, like a great rain in time of drought. And there is a certain boy born in Norwich a little before this, (I have a sad story to tell here) whose father had come from Rhode Island, and who was of a somewhat doubtful character, falling eventually into dissolute habits and poverty; but he had married a worthy woman; and the boy, as such things will happen, had inherited all of the mother's energy and none of her goodness, and all of the father's deviltry with none of his weakness; the boy's name was Benedict Arnold. I dislike to name it; but truth is truth, and history is history. He cannot stay in the drug store of the Messrs. Lathrop, where he has been placed — too bad for that. He runs away and enlists for the French war. Ah! if some friendly bullet had slain him there! But no; he is to gain manhood for a warning to all men everywhere, that courage and ambition and energy are nothing, and worse than nothing, except they be governed by an honest purpose, and tempered by a sterling humanity.

More honor to-day from us who are gathered here, to Goodman John Elderkin, who built his mill according to contract, and faithfully ground his grist, than to the great major-general Arnold, in British short clothes, and crowned with infamy. These memorial days are not the glorifiers only, they are also the avengers. If Norwich, in an awkward moment, has given birth to a villain, let us not be silent in this the day of her rejoicing, but let the world know that we are second to none in giving him our scorn.

Shall we take a glance at the town in those times — anywhere from 1750 to 1770?

The little sloop Defiance is making her trips with credit and dispatch. There is a thriving ship trade at the Landing — occasionally a fleet of twenty or thirty sail; or a stout packet — Ebenezer Fitch, commander — is up for London. There is a flourishing business with the West Indies; long teams come in from the adjoining towns, blocking up the roads in the neighborhood of the town Green, bartering their produce for West India molasses, or possibly some tight little jug of West India rum. Houses are scattered up and down, from the Landing to the up town Plain. The generous old fireplaces are not all gone by, and sitting in some corner of one of these, on a winter's night, it may happen that some traveller or sailor-man just arrived by London packet, entertains an earnest, curious company, with a story of a trip to Paris, and of the shady avenues of Versailles, and the carriages of the great king covered with gold, and fountains that throw water a hundred feet in the air! I say the fire-places are not all gone, though a certain Dr. Franklin has latterly contrived stoves, which are said to secure a wonderful economy of heat. And the same gentleman, it is whispered, in well read circles, has learned to catch the lightning and to bottle it.

Some adventurous young fellow, disposed to make a dash, is fined heavily for riding to church in a gig, and disturbing the sobriety of the congregation. The women go to church in plain homespun — good, innocent creatures, never having thought of making a personal exhibition of themselves. Ah, if good old Dr. Lord, who was preaching in that day, though he was past seventy — if good old Dr. Lord, I say, could have seen some fine woman of our time, sailing up the centre aisle, swaying along under a great breadth of silken canvas, I think he would have urged with new unction, "*strait is the gate and narrow is the way*," — that the good people follow.[1]

---

[1] The fashion of that day compelled use of stupendous hoops, or of some equivalent device for making "spread;" the allusion—as such things will—created its little breeze of applause. I particularly remember the approval of a certain quiet, bald-headed gentleman among the auditors, who

But Dr. Lord's is not the only church in these times; there has grown up below the hill a thriving little village, called Chelsea, which has its own meeting-house, and church members, not very harmonious as yet,— a certain Mr. Whitaker being the bone of a rather sharp theological contention; but who knows but the little parish may come in time to rival the mother church upon the Green?

And on the heights of Franklin, which was then but a corner of the "Nine miles square," there is another orthodox place of worship, whose quaint architecture withstood the bleak northwesters down to our own time; and I can well remember, though my memory does not run so far back as that of a good many I see about me—I can well remember, I say, treading very awe-stricken over the broad stone boulder which formed the stepping-stone, and peering through the bobbin balustrade that ran round the tops of the square pews, at the huge sounding-board, with its wonderful carving, and the gray velvet cushions of the desk; and listening to the quavering falsetto tones of the little white-haired

---

had been perspiring between two enormous heaps of silk— which permitted only his waistcoat and head to appear—and who applauded this utterance with a relish that was almost frantic.

old gentleman, in black knee-breeches, who maintained, there upon his mountain altar, to the very last, all the fire and energy of the puritan spirit.

There were two good taverns in those days upon the town green; and there was a paper mill in the valley of the Yantic, with Christopher Leffingwell, Esq., for proprietor; there was a stage coach running to Providence; there was a bridge built after long altercation over the foot of the Cove. And though it sounds like an Arabian story, I must relate to the young people of Norwich that before this period a wide expanse of water, over which an occasional ferry-boat plied, lay between John Breed's corner and the station of the New London railway. Good revolutionary feeling prevailed; the ladies giving last and sternest proof of it in abandoning their tea drinking; and the stamp act was anathematized in good set terms in open town meeting. Old Governor Trumbull used to come down, in a square-topped gig, perhaps to see his son Joseph, who lived hereabout, and to look out for his West Indian business; or, as times grew threatening, to collect ammunition, or beef or mutton for the army,—all the while writing his messages regularly,—giving good advice to his son regularly,—paying his debts regularly,—collecting his bills regularly,—attending church regularly; in short, a most capital type of the shrewdness, and energy, and piety of the old Connecticut character. A little later he entertains there upon the Lebanon green the gay Duke of Lauzun,[1] who has come over, with a generosity that is more chivalric than earnest, to help us fight out the great fight of the century.

And what a contrast it is,—this gay nobleman, carved out, as it were, from the dissolute age of Louis XV.,—who had sauntered under the colonnades of the Trianon, and had kissed the hand of the Pompadour, now strutting among the staid dames of Norwich and of Lebanon! How they must have looked at him and his fine troopers, from under their knitted hoods! You know, I suppose, his after history; how he went back to Paris, and among the wits there, was wont to mimic the way in which the stiff old Connecticut Governor had said grace at his table. Ah, he did not know that in Governor Trumbull, and all such men, is the material to found an enduring State; and in himself, and all such men, only the inflammable material to burn one down.

---

[1] *Armand-Louis Gontaut*, duc de Biron — but known in all his earlier days, and by the *Mémoires* (Paris, 1822) as *Duc de Lauzun*. He was condemned to death by the French revolutionary tribunal in 1793.

There is a life written of Governor Trumbull, and there is a life written of the *Duc de Lauzun*. The first is full of deeds of quiet heroism, ending with a tranquil and triumphant death; the other is full of rankest gallantries, and ends with a little spurt of blood under the knife of the guillotine upon the gay Place de la Concorde.

I shall not linger upon the revolutionary period, nor seek to prove that our fathers were good patriots, and, therefore, good revolutionists. I think we feel that truth sufficiently in the tingling blood which they have bequeathed to us. I go on, therefore, to glance for a moment at times which white-haired men here — and I see many — remember: — when trade had revived after the war; when turnpike roads were laid out with wonderful engineering skill straight over the tallest hills; when wagons with elliptic springs had been contrived to carry four persons with ease; when the weekly newspaper gave startling intelligence from New York not more than three days old; when the slow sailing Defiance has given place to a rakish looking, two masted craft; and when in well informed, though somewhat speculative circles, there is talk of eventually putting upon the route a vessel that should go by steam. Of course, there were prodigious shakings of the head at this, just as we shake our heads now at the talk of Mr. La Mountain or of Mr. Wise[1] (of course I speak of the Wise who puts his gas in balloons). But the steamboats come in their time; and I am sure that I address a large crowd of sympathizing auditors, now that I come to speak of the magnificent old "Fanny," spluttering and paddling, and splurging up to the little wharf under the lea of Pepper's Hill, where the pine wood lay piled in fabulous quantities. It was a rare treat in those days to drive down in a gig to Swallowall or Chelsea, and look over at the marine monster, with her smoke pipe, and her balustrade of netted ropes, and her engine of twenty-horse power more or less, and capable of driving through the United States mail in twenty-four hours. Ah, those wonders, and lifts, and joys of boyhood! There are those here, I am sure, who will pardon me the expression of them; for there are those here who have kindred memories —joys that are past; houses they knew, that are demolished; trees that sheltered them, cut down; brooks, whose murmur they loved, filled in, banked over, lost. Graves, too, which you and I remember, fresh rounded, that are sunken now; and voices low

---

[1] Messrs. La Mountain and Wise were the famous aëronauts of that day: and just at that time too, Hon. Henry A. Wise of Virginia was exasperating the public mind by inflammatory political harangues—full of wind and flame.

and tender, and loving voices which, for these many a weary year, have been silent — silent! I do not envy the man who has not such memories to-day; they make hearts touch each other as nothing else could do; and we, who come here under the cold tie of township, find suddenly breaking into life and power that nobler bond of brotherhood.

But this is a festal day; we are crowning the good year '59 with rejoicing; and in this time, is our town of Norwich doing nothing? Are the good things, and the brave things, all past things? Is it nothing,—the hum of a myriad spindles along all your water-courses, singing of industry and enterprise? Is it nothing to inaugurate the century with such temples of learning[1] as stand yonder, the monument of your private munificence? Is it nothing to show such phalanx of men as I see about me, all of whom by nativity, or citizenship, or near ties of blood, give honor to your town, and take honor?[2] Is it nothing to have given a half score of the best, and worthiest, and weightiest names to the commercial exchange of our metropolis? Is it noth-

---

[1] The allusion was to the Norwich Free School.

[2] Among those upon the platform, and in the immediate neighborhood of the speaker, were Governor Buckingham, Senator Lafayette Foster, Ex-president Fillmore, Chancellor Walworth, and the Hon. Erastus Corning of New York.

ing to have furnished the Empire state a presiding head for her great central thoroughfare; nothing to have provided them in the person of our venerable friend, with a man who honored their high office of Chancellor? Is it nothing to be represented in our national senate by a man whom you delight to honor at home? Is it nothing to have given to the world a songstress, whose melody charms, and whose virtues allure and instruct the growing mind of the whole country? Is it nothing to have loaned our little commonwealth of Connecticut — what is so rare in politics — a thoroughly upright man for Governor?

But while we boast and glorify ourselves to-day, let us remember that 'Nine-miles-square' do not bound the world, and never did. Year by year, the iron roads, and the journals, and the leashes of electric wire are binding us in the bond of a common humanity. Year by year, and century by century, special titles and special states, and special privileges, and special nationalities, are going down under the horizon, as we rise to the level of a higher, a nobler, and juster civilization. Year by year, the good, and the strong, and the true, and the hopeful, are forming more and more one great parish, whose high priest is the God of Love. Not an oppressor can lift his arm to strike, the wide world over, but the knowledge and the shame of it, riding upon the wing of lightning, shall kindle indignation in honest hearts everywhere. Only yesterday, how our bosom thrilled with the struggles, and toils, and broken hopes of those poor children of Italy, — not farther from us than the victims of Frontignac from our fathers.

And now, one last word to you who live in Norwich: You have a great trust to fill; and we, who are natives or descendants, commit it this day solemnly to your charge. There are memories here that are ours as well as yours; cherish them faithfully. There are graves here that are ours *more* than they are yours; I pray you guard them tenderly! We have hopes here, too; build them up — build them up bravely. We have a pride here. See to it, men of Norwich, that our pride and your pride — just pride — have no fall, until the rocks, and the rivers, and the plains, which are spread out here for your abode and for your delight, shall pass away.

V.

TWO COLLEGE TALKS.

1857–1882.

TWO COLLEGE TALKS.

FIRST TALK.

(In Church of the Divine Unity, 1857.)

TWENTY-FIVE years ago, when the outer eddies of this metropolis had hardly circled to the spot where we are assembled to-night, there met together in a village of Central New York, within sight of the valley of the Mohawk, and of the blue hills of Trenton, a little company of the students of Hamilton College, who counselled together how they might help themselves forward in literary and social culture, outside of the academic discipline. It seemed to them that some new graft might be set upon the native stock of the College; it seemed to them that such new graft might bear somewhat finer and juicier fruit than belonged to the parent stem. It would appear that the end justified their anticipations; and scions from this new growth, with true American enterprise, were speedily set in half the colleges of the country, where they shot up presently into permanent institutions, whose delegates have come here to-night, to celebrate an anniversary which marks the first quarter of a century.

We recognize in this society (of A Δ Φ) a type of the American want, and of the democratic demand, for Association. A few congenial spirits come together; a moderator is appointed; they discuss their needs; they establish a constitution to meet those needs; they club their funds; secretaries correspond; chapters are formed; conventions are called;—we respect the authority and obey the summons— all the more readily because it is so true an expression of the national tendency. We love associative action; it is the primordial law of our development; we crystallize normally in that shape. You cannot go so far away but you shall be enrolled in some Society—for printing campaign documents —for horticulture—for repairing churches—for building railways. It is the source of our executive energy. It makes the grand lifts along our republican level; isolated, we are but pebbles on the shore; but band us together by affinities we love and cherish, and there is a great sea-wall, over which the waters cannot come.

Our Fraternity is, I say, a type of this associative energy; and the more remarkable, perhaps, as having grown up under the wing of one of the few despotic regimes which are left to us — I mean the necessarily despotic regime of the College. The club stands related to the University, as an' expression of young Republicanism in contrast with the rigidity of old forms: As if the American instinct for associative action — for ballotings — for holding meetings — were too strong to be snuffed out utterly by the hand of discipline, and must show itself, and speak, and grow. I do not mean to imply that there is any necessary antagonism, further than the natural and healthful antagonism always existing between the fastness of young blood, and the inertia of old brains.

I suppose I may say, without infringing upon the time-honored mystery of your cabalistic Greek, that the general object of this Association, as now constituted, is a cultivation of those refinements of letters or of social feeling, which are to a certain extent ignored by the administration of the college.

Under its regimen, a somewhat larger range is given to a man's individuality of character; his special intellectual impulses are not strained to the measure of a common standard, but his tastes are granted their particular divergences. Those club-rooms were quiet alcoves, where we used to try on the harness which our masters, with their Davies, and Playfair, and Plato, were fitting to our limbs. If too loose, they were taken in there; if too tight, (which often happened,) they were loosened.

I hope I shall give no offence to the younger members of the Fraternity, when I relate with what pride those College encounters with the Gog and Magog, that go about desolating human society, were regarded by us. For myself, my blood glows even now, at the thought of some chivalrous assault in those days, with the borrowed sword of Juvenal, upon some arrant usurper in the literary world. How we mowed down whole ranks of people with a couplet of Horace! And how surprisingly all these people recovered afterward: and what very nice people we thought them when we came to live among them, and to ask favors of them! You will find there are a great many such bloodless victories outside of Colleges: a great many dismal giants who thwack terribly — but always in private.

It involves a certain degree of hardihood to advocate, now-a-days, the refinements of letters; the practical so overshadows and awes us. You and I value things very much for their palpable and manifest profit; not considering enough perhaps, what other, remoter, and larger profit may grow out of those meditations or studies, whose germinating power is slower, more delicate, and less easily traceable.

Even in Science, we rank abstract and elemental ideas below positive and practical development. The man who maps the tides or the winds so as to shorten voyages this year or next, is more estimated than the individual who spends years in determining the position of certain new stars, in establishing the niceties of longitudinal difference, or discovering some new metallic base of an old earthy matter. And yet it is possible that the star-finder may be opening an investigation which shall simplify the whole subject of navigation; or the delver in the earth — whose product is now only a new chemical fact to announce — may live to see that particular fact revolutionize a whole branch of industry. The truth that simmered for fifty years under the Voltaic pile, in all that time serving only to give a shock to nervous people, or to fuse a bit of metal, blazed out at last: And now, it plays upon an iron web from city to city, over the world; frail as the gossamer things we see on a summer's morning, pendant from grass-tip to grass-tip — swaying in every breath of air — and yet, the bridges of thousands of airy messengers who carry their errands, and die.

So too, I think there is something in a refined intellectual cultivation, and its processes, which, though it seems to lack practical relation, will blaze out some day in subtle flame, from many a man's mind and heart — refining character and action, and justifying itself by various and rich accomplishment.

Seeing, therefore, that certain special literary culture is one of the chiefest ends of your Fraternity, let us consider some of the aspects of literary endeavor at the present day; what changes have come over it during those twenty-five years which end tonight; what new tastes we have to deal with, and how these concern us, or we them.

First, we remark the antagonism which is growing up between the merely classical aspects of Education and its present demands; between the reformers and the dilettanti. The living languages are urged in place of the dead; and the natural sciences in place of pure mathematics. M. Guizot and DeTocqueville are more eagerly read, than Cicero de Officiis; their authority is counted greater than that of any of the old statists. Mr. Grote is steeping us in Greek color and Greek sympathy, (with his earnest humanitarian and Christian philosophy superadded,) as Thucydides and Herodotus have lost the power to do; and Niebuhr has plucked all the marrow from Livy's hard, dry, glittering anatomy of Rome.

It is more than suspected that the pretty Greek sepulchres, like sepulchres everywhere, contain a vast deal of deadness and of rottenness; the classicists indeed argue for that eclectism of taste which finds suggestive material wherever there is force and beauty; and Milton assures us that a good man, like Athanasius, could out of the slime of Aristophanes dredge the matter for a rousing sermon. But Athanasius was no undergraduate; who, it is thought, would be much safer with the nebulæ of Herschel than with those of Strepsiade and Cherephon.

There is no fear, however, that past good things will be lost, although they may be supplanted in educational systems by the more lively new things. Good things and beautiful things do not die easily. They belong so far to the spirit and complexion of succeeding literature, that the curious, and all loving scholars will be constantly upon their track. If the student's thought is diverted to observation, measurement, and classification of those new geometric figures which belong to mineral crystallization, we still regard the charming clearness of Euclid's demonstrations as so many outline drawings, which the mind dwells upon with a certain artistic pleasure : and if we quote Homer no more, we hang his Frog-piece upon our walls, as a dainty cabinet picture, and harmonious bit of ancient coloring.

Growing out of this antagonism, or at the least coincident with it, we note the every-day practical tone, which has latterly come to pervade literature generally.

Twenty-five years ago, and poor Sir Walter Scott was touching with his palsied, but beloved hand, the last gleams of that feudal splendor that shone from the corselet of Count Robert of Paris. Sharon Turner had, at about the same time, closed the old series of English Histories with his cumbrous quartos, which I believe everybody speaks well of, and nobody reads. Since that date, I think you can rarely fail to have observed a more intimate alliance of all literary endeavor — growing every hour closer and closer — with the wants of our every-day life, and its thorough incorporation with live things. The scholar, the romancist, the scientific man, are no longer a company apart. Their aims and records are of what we know and feel, and live by ; or they are shelved as curious specimens of vain work — Chinese carving, showing infinite detail of labor perhaps, but wanting the perspective and foreshortening which make them true, and which body forth life.

Mere metaphysics is dead. Chivalric tales, with however much of rhetorical spice in them, do not flame in our hearts, and kindle love there, and joy and wonder. Science must buckle itself to cloth-weaving or printing, or its story does not reach. Searchers after lost asteroids give way to the man, who with his magnetic battery, touches our fire-bells with curious, invisible stroke. The Doctors have, I think, given over the formulas of an old-time theology, for a preaching that swoops down on the bad things we do; and not upon the possible bad things we might think, if we thought as somebody long ago is supposed to have thought.

Dickens slays your niggardness and mine, with his cheery Christmas legends. There is no Jack the Giant-Killer — no bean stalk and castles; but, the Circumlocution office, Foggy Chancery, and the man we all know so well — imposing Mr. Gradgrind.

What hope indeed to be read or listened to, if we do not point our thought where the world's thought is pointing? We may sing a sweet song: but will people stay to listen? A few very sweet — a Maud, a Hiawatha — may cheat us into a wayside delay; but these are exceptional. A rude campaign rhyme ringing with the jingle and clatter of to-day's march, may go even wider. Novels are writ full of some moral drawn from yesterday's news; the imaginative man or woman must yoke themselves to the great processional advance, or their fine fancies and they are trampled down and forgotten.

Compare Household Words with the Spectator, and you will see at a glance the difference I would bring to your notice. We do not absolutely give up our old friends, Will Honeycomb, Sir Roger, and the rest;—we cherish their memories warmly; but they are thoroughly dead friends. If you try to make them live again, they will be ghosts only; the world will laugh at your pets and their short clothes; a single paragraph in a morning paper will blow them into limbo.

So Dr. Primrose, that charming old gentleman whom we love, as we love a good family portrait— even Dr. Primrose is growing seedy. I doubt if our followers upon negro minstrelsy could be brought to laugh at Jenkins, or Moses, and his gross of spectacles. We have lived up to that level, and passed it by. The new excisemen take no cognizance of the gooseberry wine; it is drawn too mild. The Vicar of Wakefield is not a tract any longer; it is only history.

The great literary caravan has trailed away from that pleasant country where the woods were soft and low; where meadows lay green around homely places; where morning larks soared from the dewy herbage, in serenest light and bubbled songs; where gray hamlets lay scattered on the earth's bosom like children sleeping, and the parish bells woke from the hills holy lullabys. All this is left; and the processional advance is under hot suns, with a harsh level around us; where there is din and crash — swords of adventurers, new harems by the Salt Lake — tawny slave faces — stealthy murders, and murderers who sneer at, and balk us. They who are joined to that march under the intense atmosphere of to-day, cannot dally and snuff at flowers.

The five millions of readers and thinkers in America, feeling citizen rights — eager to establish families in comfort, if not in opulence — all of them heated by the fever of activity, want to give time and attention only to what concerns them nearly — their relations to each other and the State; something present, practical, and vital. They have no leisure for the vague, the insubstantial, the apocryphal. A literature to reach them, and inoculate their thoughts, must be directed toward those grand topics, or seasoned with that large humanity which concerns all; there must be something which is aired with life as they breathe it, and with freedom as they feel it. Your book — your treatise on popular astronomy, your poem, if you please — your views on the judiciary — your discussion of music — your tale, has not found final judgment with respect to its fitness as an American document, till it has gone far out three thousand miles west of the sea, to the lands of new settlers, who lay your argument or your fancies, like a plummet, to the stature of their mental need; who test it by that much of hope, of fulness, of joy, it adds to their inner life.

And now, seeing that literature and its aims have been drawing nearer to our every-day habit of thought, during these past twenty-five years; — seeing that the atmosphere of books is less remote than it was, and extreme classicism withdrawn to a more frigid distance than ever before, it may be worth our while to enquire how we (who, as members of a literary fraternity, may be supposed to have some sort of literary labor in prospect) stand affected by the change?

Is cultivation like classicism, out-marched? Is the standard lowered? Or is it, that the horizon is only extended, since readers and thinking men all, have come up to a higher level of observation?

I think you will readily agree with me that there was never a time, when there was need for more thorough and various cultivation than now. It may not indeed be the same sort of cultivation which once obtained. It may matter little to you to distinguish between the Ionic and Doric forms of speech; matter little if you know whether Cicero plead for, or against the poet Archias; matter little how much of Horace is in Sapphic — how much in Iambic measure; but it may matter greatly to you to know, when Horace — if you read him — came near to that truth about men, and men's lives and passions, which never dies. It may matter nothing to know if Æneas or Turnus be the proper hero of Virgil's Epic; but it may matter greatly to know, when and by what illustrations he may have drawn a real hero — defending real rights, full of a real humanity; or only a mock hero, who dies with the clang which an honest blow will ring, and ring again upon the shield of every pretender: we want that sort of cultivation which will enable its possessor to distinguish between sham and substance — between the true and the false — the things which help us really, and the things which brilliantly seem to.

The literary man differs from others only in this: — he puts in words what others put in action. His cultivation must apply itself to what is near to us — near our wants — near to our hope. The oaks stand by their own vigor, fed from their falling leaves; the grain that shot up last spring-time wants your care. You may find implements in classic stock, in old armories, where the glitter and order attract you; but you have more to deal with than the blotches of rust, at which the classic conservators weary themselves, with file and acid.

Your labor, if it is to tell, must tell other-wheres — your blows fall outside, on living wrongs — wrongs that scream at the touch.

Again, there must be habit of close and unremitting observation, wide wakefulness — a finger always upon the world's pulse. And to this end it is quite essential to a literary worker who is thoroughly in earnest, that he keep his station near to the heart of things. He must think much in cities. He must imbibe the movement where movement is strongest. That concentration which is effected amidst the turmoil of the world, strikes straight and sharp to its aim; but the concentration which comes of quietude, belongs to a pleasantly rarefied medium, and never gains the focal energy which burns things to their core.

The outside observer may appreciate and enjoy — all the more strongly — because there is a constant calm about him. But he cannot from his outpost reach the centres effectively with either pen or tongue. He lives too slowly. People scent his rusticity a long way off. Quick as he may get the current of history, by steam or telegraph, in the very moment when it turns from him back toward the centre, the arterial briskness is lost : it is heavy, sluggish, venous. It needs airing ; it must come to the great lungs of cities and seaports.

But while the practical literary tendency of the day is, in a certain sense, antagonistic to an old and elegant classicism, I would not imply that it is utterly vagrant; indeed, it was never subordinated to a more thorough and searching criticism than now. It may not be tried by the antique standards. The drama we act is not judged by any effete law of the unities, but by its present Power.

Are the men, men? Are the women, women? These are the questions we ask of whatever representations of life our artists, preachers, authors set before us. Do the things they accomplish lie within our reach? Next, do they lie in the path of our duty? This is the basis, I think, of most of modern criticism ; indeed, it is the natural result of that practical drift of the intellectism of our day, to which I have called your attention. We are going back nearer and nearer to the elemental principles of art. We are flinging off allegiance to conventional standards; we are less attracted by the glitter of any feudal harness, and want to see the muscle, and nerve, and heart of the man who wears it. Horace Walpole, with his dim Otranto, is less now than Mr. Mayhew with his Poor of London.

Some eighteen months ago, you listened from these same benches to the great satirist[1] of our time, as he laid before you his gallery of historic pictures. How intently you watched, as he sketched the shadowy trifles, the every-day weaknesses, the talk, the banter, the follies of a Royal household! And yet it was for no pomp of description that you gave your minds to him; but for the exceeding truth and penetration with which he probed to the very marrow of their manhood — the royal subjects — tore away every kingly illusion, and set before you *the men.*

But not only are our critical estimates broader and deeper, but in the last twenty-five years we have made great gains in all that pertains to æsthetic culture. In art proper, we see the tendency toward elemental bases of opinion, in the existence and growth of the Pre-Raphaelite doctrine. This may be an extravagance; but it is an extravagance in the right direction; it is toward simplicity and truth.

I think the humors of such classic sticklers as Le Brun, and even Poussin, have given way to a manner and treatment that storm our sensibilities, with no lance held in classic poise, no fanfaronade of gauntlets and trumpets, but only quiet, truthful nature.

---

[1] The allusion is to Thackeray and his lectures on the "Four Georges."

I think that in our Academy Gallery we are having every year less and less of impossible Strephons and Clorindas; less of Miss Languish, and more of the material we look for in wives and daughters. I think the scenic pastorals, with their twin cows, orderly trees, and pretty water, are giving way to the meadows we know and love—to the mountains that dwarf us, and kindle worship.

Of course there are platitudes still; men who, with rare appreciation, lack the *summa manus*, the *vis manutigii*. But the intention of our art is becoming far more earnest. It is running toward those essentials, and directed by those maxims which give it a universal character.

A book or a picture may have a conventional charm, which will give it admirers, just now and here; but only real trees, real water, real men, real passion, will please those who come in from without, or who belong to a generation after us.

And here, in connection with our art-tendencies, I cannot forbear to mention a name, which I am sure you all know and respect; I mean that of John Ruskin, who is thoroughly a man of our time, and a bold type of that amalgamation of æsthetic aims with our life and every-day endeavor, at which I have hinted.

He has done more than any man to bring the

literature of art from its vagueness and shadowy region, and to make out its determination by certain fixed principles. And in so doing he has torn away no grace from the artist-life, but rather sublimed it, by the union which he has demonstrated between its offices and our religion and faith, and all that we reverence in truth and beauty everywhere.

There is another noticeable thing about Mr. Ruskin, which I feel sure has made his name a welcome one to thoughtful Young America. He is always in earnest. He glows everywhere: the track of him is dyed deeply with his soul's life. Whether he flames into grandiloquence, or stays you with his dogged iteration, he is aboundingly and gushingly full of the matter in hand. He has no half-feelings, or half-thoughts; all are rounded with the swell of a deep, devotional tide.

He winds into his subject, whether painting or temple, like a serpent; and though you may lose his trail because you lack his enthusiasm, you may be sure that he is winding his way up through columns, through colors, through domes; and you shall see, by and by, in token of his progress, some gorgeous pennant of his rhetoric streaming from the top.

The progress of æsthetic culture is to be seen moreover in other directions than in that of plastic art. It is to be noted in our quickened perception and appreciation of the beauties of music, in our deeper and more enlightened understanding of its principles : — in our nicer distinction between those sounds which play melodiously about the ear, and those others, which with fulness and density of meaning, gravitate to the soul, and make inner symphonies *there*.

In all our mechanic arts, we may observe a shrewd trade-perception of harmony of parts, and grace of form. Manufacturers find their profit in employing artists to design their patterns; and the cheapest prints are nine-penny illustrations of Owen Jones' theory of color.

Typography has made vast strides ; not only is there advance in the mere mechanism, but in the general taste which presides over the art of bookmaking. What would be thought now of those pitiful annuals and souvenirs, with their lack-a-daisical faces, and pretty, impossible park scenes, which, twenty years ago, we gave to young Misses in leg-of-mutton sleeves, as tokens of tender and respectful affection? Does any body give them, or print them now? How poorly these would show beside that story of Darley's Margaret, in which the genius of the artist has startled a dead author from his grave.

How the whole art of wood-engraving has flashed out into piquancy and grace, carrying fulness and completeness of detail! How we look out for things we wondered about; faces of men we hear of, and seem to get at something real — feeding our curiosity and art-love together.

Again, those wonderful sun-light pictures, bringing the rarest bits of landscape, and the infinite detail of Moorish or Venetian architecture to our study tables; what quickeners and cultivators of our taste in this direction have these become! A portfolio now is as good as a year's travel.

Our homes, again, whether we will or not, give tokens of our artistic longings, in their graceful adaptations for our comfort. Your very pottery is taking on forms of the best Etruscan art, and you pour your tea from some duplicate of the wine-pot of Sallust.

And how widely, and how tenderly this æsthetic spirit has breathed over those other homes, where our ambitions, and rivalries, and earnestness all end at last. There may be even here, sometimes, tasteless blazon of marble — ostentation clamoring against the silence; but we forgive it for the love that shines in it; and as for the trees, the flowers, the sheltering vines, thank God! these are never tasteless. They bind up a holy and fragrant alliance of all that is beautiful without, with all that is hopeful within; and to you, to me, to all whose memories run ever to those silent places, the flowers, and vines, and trees, must bring with every repeated season, a tenderly repeated promise, that the dead will not be always dead.

We observe then, with respect to the literary tendencies of the day, that they are characterized by a vital earnestness; that their aims are present and active, not reflective and abstract. We observe, that our past habit of American life has impressed itself upon the whole tone of intellective action; and we can bridle its swiftness by no classic erudition, by no mere educational dogmas. We cannot bridle it at all. Guide it, however, we may, by that wakeful and thorough cultivation, which, without ignoring popular extravagances, is no way blinded by splendid falsities; and which reckons up the value of your poem or mine, your picture or mine, your sermon or mine — not by any laws of old schools, not by any theologic dogmas, but by the simple, earnest, hearty, helpful truth, that may shine there.

I will not close without bringing to notice, that other aim of your association, which looks to social improvement. I think we are needy in that way —

most of all at an educational age. We want something to defeat, or rather qualify that old, hard bookishness which once belonged, and was thought necessary to every scholarly man; something to make him supple; something to give pliancy to nerve and adroitness to strength.

I think I am not mistaken in supposing the Fraternity wakeful to that good which lies in a good manner, uniting kindliness with ease. The man of the cloister cannot meet the every-day want, until he has taken on somewhat of the every-day pliancy and aptitude. Without it he chafes at his unfitness, perhaps consoles himself with the barren thought of possessing weightier truth, fuller knowledge, deeper insight than the man of the world. But that world-knowledge, which gives a tongue to learning, which supplies the magnetism of look and presence, and which ensures confidence in action, is no way inconsistent with large acquirement. No man can be thoroughly practical — up to the level of American requirement — who does not constantly and habitually bring his attainments, however various they may be, to the test of outside — every-day — familiar discussion and analysis.

And here I may take occasion to say, that there is, or was a scholastic stiffness, which preserved itself and fed itself, by sneering at the opinions or the criticism of such society as is enlivened by the graces of women. In our world of equal condition, where the great social conservator is the respect we habitually show to the other sex, nothing could be weaker or more ill-judged. You may distrust at once the manly aptitude and thorough cultivation of that individual, who whatever his boasts or professions may be, sneers at the opinions of intelligent women.

Nor do I think that your scholastic prig really entertains the contempt he may affect. He finds it hard to break down or to break through his retirement and the reticence of his desk-life. He feels an irritating sense of his inaptness to carry his learning gracefully into the social arena, and soothes his mortified vanity with the prettiness of a sarcasm. This might do for the old-fashioned schoolmasters; but it is too late now. Too many princes of learning, too many veterans of science are among us, familiarly, illustrating by manner, and by talk, the fulness of their accomplishment, and the modesty of real attainment. We cannot worship any longer the scholarship which enthrones itself in seclusion, and wears only the clumsy buckram of books.

Again, a friendliness and good-fellowship spring out of the club-socialities of college, which we need to keep and carry with us. We republicans are prone to a harsh kind of social disintegration. We associate for furtherance of scientific, political, religious aims; but we do not bring our affections to the compact. Even kinship does not hold us together. We need certain rallying channels wherein our kindly feelings may group themselves, and recover their electrical forces by attrition.

Older countries possess in their castes and clanships, in their ancestral attachments and common pride, constant promoters of fellow-feeling, as between those of the same classes. We lack all this: we carry our independence as citizens into a kind of cold, isolating indifference. We are constantly forcing our equality into an impertinent assertion of manner that outrages fellowship; as if making one's self disagreeable were upon the whole the best possible way of saying, "I am as good as you!"

I pray you, gentlemen, frown on this! It is common, and it is despicable. A great many ardent boasters of our institutions are nervously anxious under the social juxtaposition which belongs to their development. They are sighing to make themselves exceptional; haunted with the phantom of some social superiority, which shall be so marked as to sting outsiders into acquiescence. That man who is constantly fretting, lest he be not made enough of, either intellectually or socially, had better set himself to find some surer position both ways.

I am afraid we have made our most sorry figure abroad, by this undue insistance on our *status;* a too quick scent for imagined affronts; as if a man could be any thing less than he really is, except he himself give cause. A simple republican citizen! that any man should chafe at that, who has American blood in his veins, or try to round it into something over-decorous; something whereby he may astonish, and make the ignorant ones gape, and the cultivated smile. Have we not a national sore of this sort which needs caustic and excoriation?

After all, what a world of impertinences, ill-manners, affectations, would pass away from us, if only we would accept that oldest, simplest, best law of good-fellowship, — about being kind to others, as we would have others kind to us! Is there not room under this for republican manhood to dilate and take stature and dignity?

There is a virtue in those little every-day courtesies of man to man, of which we are nationally forgetful. They dignify each one's sense of his personality; they stimulate the moral health of the nation; they carry a cheery glow everywhere; they make a constant, unnoticed, teeming sunshine — a stray gleam here, and a stray gleam there — but in the aggregate, making a great harvest swell.

We admire splendid and startling charities, but ignore the lesser ones, which give a right social *animus* to life. I think there are American names associated with great simple acts of beneficence, which I should need only to mention to call down plaudits. We yield all the length and depth of our sympathy in the applause, and think it a good deed in us — well over. We go out to forget our own way-side, social charities — of indulgence, forbearance, regard for others, a day-long and life-long living up toward the level of our plaudit.

How our hearts yearned toward that fair English woman, who crossed seas to give comfort amid the Turkish war-scenes! Had she come hither, I hardly dare say what might have been the expression of our admiration. I think we should have dragged her carriage through our streets. I am afraid we should have forgotten all in some municipal imbroglio. I fear we should not have funded our admiration in any great hospital endowment. They have done this, you know, over seas. How august and grand — it seems to rise amid the fog and smoke of London — soaring in the eye of faith, higher than any Victoria tower — that monument of a tender beneficence, wherein children's voices, for generations and generations, shall call down blessings on the name of Florence Nightingale.

And yet you — if I might venture a word outside of the Fraternity — you who have brought your womanly smile and countenance to cheer us here to-night, can act the charity over: can graft all its nobility, if not its notice, upon your social intercourse — in ever so little kindnesses — regard for the wishes and feelings of others — a constant leaven of charity, which will make duty rise to nobleness.

And you, gentlemen of the Fraternity, remember that we have other brothers in the world beside those of our Society: do not forget — do not limit good-fellowship.

The literary and social league which ties us together, is, after all, but the educational programme of something to do in life. You will easily slip away — easier than you now think — from the specialities of this College alliance; — be out of the range of its provisions — be engrossed with quite other interests. It will seem to you — as I venture to say it seemed to me — but a rich vine hiding the roughness of the old walls which once sheltered us, and nodding welcome from its leaves of green.

But let the faith and courage its exercises may have taught, go with you. Remember that there is a degree of swift vitality in this American world of ours, which calls for something more than the slow processes of schools — or the severity of classicism — which demands the practical, the earnest, the helpful. But though the classicism you love may be outrun — holding place only like the shrined saints on Papish road-side, whereat votaries bow, say prayers, and hurry on — remember that cultivation of other kinds is still demanded: that a judgment refined by much study still presides over all that is well done: that an enlightened criticism will attend you — quick to the necessities of the hour, and based upon those enduring and substantial principles of art, which pervade all thinking minds at this day.

Remember, that the taste which is expressing itself in ever new and improving forms all around us, will have its measure upon your accomplishment.

Remember, we have this great scheme of Republicanism to carry out in our lives — to keep warm in our hearts. All its contrasts — its wantings — its hardnesses — its stains are ours, as truly as its spread and its promise.

Live up to the level of your best thought; keep the line of your life tense and true; it is but a thread; but it belongs to the great Republican warp, where Time is weaving a Nation. You cannot alter its attachment yonder, to the past — nor yonder, to the unrolling years. The shuttle of to-day is flying swift — knitting blotches — knitting beauties; and if you would broider such things there as will stand fast, and carry your name worthily upon the roll of history, you will have need of all your Energy to dare — of all your Cultivation to refine — of all your Charity to ennoble.

SECOND TALK.

(At Academy of Music, New York, 1882.)

TWENTY-FIVE years have lapsed again, since at the order of this Society, I spoke before your convention of the Literary growth of the previous quarter of a century: and now — when I ought by the privileges of age to be a listener and not a talker — I am called on to add twenty-five more years to that tale of Letters, and to compass the whole story within a quarter of an hour.

I cannot do it: I cannot put the vintage of half a century into a quart-flagon. No man can.

I can only give such glimpse as you and I and all of us might have, if whirled at railway speed through the pleasant interval of Letters stretching from the year 1832 — or thereabout — to our date to-night — looking out with swift glances upon a few salient objects, and at the end of this whirl of vision having only a vague sense (perhaps sufficient for such a time of jubilee) of the drift and trend of the Interval we had hurtled over.

I seem to see — far away — about the time your Association was founded — in the wilds of Central New York — bright young fellows, by the light of whale-oil lamps, and seated on hard-bottomed benches regaling themselves with the Dandyism of Bulwer's Pelham, and wondering overmuch at the versatility of parts which could achieve a History of Athens, and set Rienzi upon his legs amidst the turmoil of decaying Rome, and put color and pulse and passion into the dry bones of Richelieu. And yet the Dandyism of Bulwer is forgettable, when we think what Exemplar he was to young men all through his life; of that System, and Industry, which alone make work *tell*.

I recal too how collegians of that date, looked out longingly through recitation-room windows, to catch glimpse of the two horsemen of Mr. G. P. R. James, as they rose above our literary horizon — steadily as the tides.

Byron was dead : but had left a fiery trail, whereat we of New England birth and breeding looked in a maze of wonder and dread. Scott we mourned for differently, and gathered with all the world in company, to throw flowers upon his fresh grave at Dryburgh.

We thought it wise to read Wordsworth, then at the pinnacle of his fame : So it was wise; So it is wise : wiser maybe, than it is winning. For the regret must ever attach, I think, to this venerated name, that he who bore it lacked the critical sagacity or the hardy courage to condemn and strip away his own redundancies — whether of fluffy languor, or homely iteration, and by so doing, to leave in bold and conquering relief such graces as made his odes cumulative with poetic splendors, and such far-reaching spiritual insight, as carries some of his utterances above all the brilliant levels of Dryden or Pope — far up amongst the Miltonian heights of song.

Christopher North we young fellows swore by, in that day. There was a breeziness, and a vigor in him, and a broad-shouldered, devil-may-care audacity that extorted our Bravos ; alas, all gone now! and aside from a few witty lunges of the *Noctes Ambrosianæ*, nothing seems left but a far-away, tinkling clamor of echoing vocables amongst the Highland Lochs.

Chiefest of critics about those times was Jeffrey : Gifford and Lockhart and Southey coming hard after : but what a king we counted Jeffrey — who, in his Edinboro Review, by a half score of pages —

had made and unmade the reputation of Poets, and Historians, and Metaphysicians! So apt — so witty — so ready — so knowing in all the Literary appetites of men and women, with not a compeer in the wide world — except it might be our own Professor of Literature.

To think, now, — that such a pretty band-box of a man could put to the shiver, such another as Thomas Carlyle! We have no such King of Criticism now; we have outlived that monarchism; our kings are in high schools, and on college benches; the critical instinct — under much and wide schooling, has shot up into a vagrancy that possesses us all. Here and there some heroic expert puts on the old lion-like ways, and growls fiercely, and snarls to the life ; but if we look hard enough we shall find jackal shanks sticking out under the lion's skin.

I named Carlyle : He too grew quickly into a deity of our young heaven, when he painted his brother poet Burns, walking —

> "In glory and in joy
> Behind his plough, upon the mountain side!"

It was only a few years before the beginnings of this Society when he blazed out in the Edinboro and Foreign Reviews. I remember well the prim green covers of the first Boston edition of his Miscellany

— bringing rich meat to our hard college commons. And for fifty years on, he kept ringing out his fierce challenge to shams and untruths—warring on Tradition, yet loving defiantly the Tradition of old-fashioned kingship: Sneering at orthodoxies and carrying a theologic back-bone as stiff as Calvin's; hirsute, rough, uncombed, grim as the wastes of his own moorland by Dumfries; but withal having a savage, uncourteous honesty in him, which is so much better than a courteous dishonesty.

They tell us he was not a model husband: Well,— who among us is? Indeed, there was not much place in him for tenderness; only that sweetest tenderness with which he followed to the last with messages of love and affection that old Scotch mother of his, who milked the cows in the Byre of Scots-Brig. Who shall say that these last fifty years are not over-much the richer for his life? Under all his convolutions of speech, that weary us, and his petulancies that tease us, and his roughness that maddens us, there is a fire slumbering which does not go down. This great Galleon upon the sea of literature has left a broad, boiling wake behind him; and all the traffickers in critical lore, and all the orthodox trimmers traversing his path as they will — for pleasure or for pains — can never wipe out the glow of its phosphorescence.

I cannot forget in this kaleidoscopic show of ours, that as early as 1833 Tennyson first gathered a budget of his young poems, which caught the sneers of the New-Timon; and which with rare exceptions had no quality beyond the millinery of Literature. But through these fifty years past, how bravely and steadily, grade by grade — illustrating in his own career the literary progress of the times — has he wrought on to that fulness of power, by which he has wrested the old Arthurian Legends from the lax hands of Geoffrey, and Map and Wace and Layamon, and brought the old British worthies to life once more, amongst the green meadows of Camelot!

Camelot was hard by Glastonbury; and that name recals the richest days of the old church in England — toward whose Traditions, John Henry Newman had eyes reverently turned, when with the devout Keble of the Christian Year, and the elder Froude, he joined in those Oxford "Tracts for the Times," which a little less than fifty years ago, kindled an ecclesiastic war in England whose angry din buzzed about our ears in the colleges. What came of it, we cannot stay to tell. But the name of Cardinal Newman is one that this age will not easily let die. So pure a heart; so keen a mind; master of that best Rhetoric which shows thought through it, as we see faces through glass — monastic in his severities — most tender of conscience — shivering for years in the winds of Doctrine, and riding up at last into the harbor of that ancient Trans-Alpine Church, where so many fine old hulks lie moored — waiting — waiting for the rise of some new Mediæval Tide.

There, too, at Oxford we encounter the Apostle of so many new Dogmas in art — whose "Lamps of Architecture" first showed their splendors some forty years ago : — earnest, indefatigable, headstrong — he too, blown about in these latter years by strange gusts of Doubt — always eloquent — tangled somewhiles in the meshes of his own tropical Rhetoric — petulant, rash : But what if — in the impatient speech of his *Clavigera* — he would tear up Railways, and burn New York? What if doubtful prophets come in his name, whose food is sunflowers and Wilde[1] honey? Let us have "Patience" — young gentlemen : let us have "Patience"! And let us remember, that back of all Ruskin's teachings, and for a testimony which can never be

---

[1] Just at this time, Mr. Oscar Wilde, the apostle of Æstheticism, was making his triumphal march, under lead of D'Oyley Carte; the same astute manager also carried to success in that day (by a sort of double campaign), Mr. Gilbert's play of Patience — which with its musical tric-trac and its plush-y pertinences, delighted everybody.

shaken, stands the beauty of the flowers, and of the clouds, and of the everlasting hills.

There are other typical Englishmen I should like to speak of — Freeman and Green putting new faces upon old English history — Matthew Arnold, widening the outlook, and deepening the grounds of intelligent criticism; and Scientists — chiefest among them that old man[1] who has just passed away in his quiet Kentish home — putting such quality in their reports of discoveries as gives literary charm — frightening the timid maybe, by the new cross lights which seem to flame athwart the Heavenly order; but which as the eye becomes used to them, lose their defiant glare, and blend — like Galileo's heresies of old — in that great trail of Light and Law which testify to the infinite Power that shaped the beginnings of things, and which will surely shape their ends — " rough hew them how we will."

And what now of our side the water? Has there been gain since the days when dear old Mr. Irving was furbishing up his stories of Granada and the Alhambra, and Cooper putting his Leather-stocking on his last tramp through the wilderness?

All of the deeps of Hawthorne lie between. And, since — in the field of Fiction, such wide blossom-

---

[1] Darwin.

ing of persistent, and of half-hardy flowers, that I cannot name them. I note only a prevailing tendency — as in other Art — to lavish skill upon technique, and minute touches that give vraisemblance — so deftly done, that the record beguiles, enchants, and makes us forget we want the story which we hardly find.

How proud we oldish people were — in college days — of the flowing smoothness and dainty scholarship which went to the making of Prescott's Histories; and how much prouder we should have been of the more masculine handling, and larger range which Motley gave to his studies of the Netherlands. Here, too, within three days last past, our octogenarian friend Mr. Bancroft, the Historian of the United States, has crowned his labors with a story of the Federal Constitution — putting to it, though years hang heavy on him — all his old conscience and vigor. Nor can I forbear to mention in this presence, that old Poet, whose Homeric head came so often to the front in New York assemblages — who wrote of Ulysses, as Homer might have written, if he had lived at Roslin and edited the *Post*; and who so filled these last fifty years with zeal, and good work as to be an exemplar to every ambitious young American.

By the same token, we may well join to night in flinging our tributary flowers upon the grave of that other Poet, whose "Voices of the Night" first streamed like a meteor across our literary firmament in the days when we elderly people of the platform were wearing our badges with Greek initials.

He loved traditions — perhaps overmuch; but he spangled them with gold of his own coinage; and he so wrought through half a century — with such balance of literary judgment — such exactitude of scholarship — such delicate ear for rhythm — such guilelessness of purpose — such reverence for all sacred and all beautiful things, as to make of his career one long, melodious " Psalm of Life."

And then — that other, whose grave is even fresher there in Concord; he a poet too; not leaning on rhythm, but making rhythm bend to his thought; — called a Philosopher, but last in all the world to call himself so : called an Idealist, yet loving more than most men home-spun words and home-spun ways. Gentlest of men, yet chafing like a lion if harnessed to creeds; full of learning that only showed by leakings he could not help; stalwart as a knight of old where wrong confronted him — in all else, as yielding as a woman.

Emerson hated impostures, much as ever Carlyle; but unlike the Scotchman he was wary and conciliatory. He could twinkle his eye winningly, as Carlyle never would, or could. He was sagacious, placable, kindly, and withal saying things in a short, *dense* way, that compels a halt, and a wrestle with them — if not acceptance; and if acceptance, then a vital acceptance that thenceforth colors life and character.

Many another amongst the living, whom we love and honor I would like to name : but I forbear: and in conclusion note only among other aspects of our present literary outlook, the vast increase of intelligent readers, which has given great quickening to literary work. There can be no good talk, except there be good listeners: these carry higher and higher the plane of literary accomplishment; not indeed gauging the volcanic peaks genius will throw up through the crusted level of average work, but making and keeping this average level better and worthier.

Compare our Journalism to-day, with that of fifty years ago, and you will see my meaning. There is reach, and grace, and pliancy, and force, where there was stolid statement only and narrow captiousness.[1]

---

[1] While paying this tribute to the larger intellectual resources at the service of the Press, there is room for doubt if there has been corresponding growth in *morale;* — doubt if the potent influences of railway magnates, of corporations, of traveling showmen, of enterprising managers — musical or histrionic — do not modify newspaper opinions, to the exclusion of old-time honesty.

Again, there is everywhere a cosmopolitan largeness belonging to all literary endeavor; unyielding creeds do not cramp utterance; conflicting beliefs march good-naturedly, side by side; divers colors of thought blend with æsthetic harmonies.

Between the same covers, lie fellow essays in easy companionship, and yet of such monstrous antagonism, as fifty years ago would have exploded, and set the paper on fire. Honest opinions, of whatever sort, do not now need the nursing and coddling of sectaries. They stand — for what they are worth, and if they do not stand, they lie. You may be sure of a pulpit and a hearing, if you have somewhat to say: and if you have nothing to say, you can get a hearing — for once.

Then, I note the wonderful accession to the supply of Young People's wants: — such school-books — such engravings — such journals — such helps at every hand — such tender companionship in colleges.

Ah, if we had possessed these in our callow days!

Again there is the Copyright Question — international and other — taking what seems shape of faint promise; as if at last — at last, the world were waking up to the notion that it is as bad a thing to rob an author — as it is to rob a grocer.

Young gentlemen, there is a fair and a most

promising field before you. Who can doubt that this Fraternity with its embranchments in so many colleges will furnish a large quota of those who will be responsible for the reach Literature shall make in the twenty-five or fifty years to come?

Some happier talker, at some happier Centennial of the future, will — maybe — have some of your names to broider upon his Legend of the great Workers. Let the hope of this, and the belief of this tingle in your blood to-night!

Let it keep you wakeful to all honorable duties. Let it make you bold, and honest, and painstaking. Let it nerve you to shun affectations — to hate shams — to love truth — to cherish simplicity: and then — whatever may betide — you will walk with a freer, and a more elastic step toward the gates, where we must all go in.

VI.

IN-DOORS AND OUT OF DOORS.

A Quatrain.

IN-DOORS AND OUT OF DOORS.

Fires and Fireside.

THE gray of a winter's morning, — so gray, as it comes through the eastern panes, that it shows only dimly the scattered books and papers of yester-night's reading, — so gray that the raked-up coals of last night's fire, as I draw them forth, glow like a heap of rubies, — a great nestling company of red jewels which will give flame of adornment to the whole day. A certain degree of art went to the making of the old wood fire; first, in the lap of ashes and against the chimney was to be coyly placed the great back-log. This might be green; it might be oak, it might be elm or pepperidge; at least it should be round, and with its bark intact; upon its top, and lying snugly between its upward swell and the advancing throat of the chimney should be placed a second bit of unsplit tree-trunk, one-half the bigness of the supporting log below; a third, of even smaller diameter,—what time a biting northeaster made demand for grand proportions,—was placed as a crowning finish upon the pair of back-logs already in position.

Then came the careful posturing of the great fire-dogs firmly against this wall of wood, spreading somewhat as they stood sturdily upon the hearth, but yet so near together as to give unquestioned support to the great forestick of cleft hickory,—a quartered bole,—with its flat side snugly settled upon the black fire-dogs. A gap of six inches—or of ten, if the outside roar called for a great mass of flame—was next to be filled in with two or three round hickory cudgels, between whose interstices free circulation would be given to fan the coals, which (the next thing in order) were piled upon the wood. Then light kindlings that crinkled with the heat, even as one placed them adroitly athwart the glowing coals; and as the smoke thickened and grew denser, the fire-maker piled on more and more of hickory saplings, of stout sticks, of cleft wood,— higher and higher, hotter and hotter, criss-crossed, with great air gaps, lightly as a child's cob-house,— fuming and steaming with the sulking heat of the ruby remnants of last night's fire-logs, until with a sudden whisk, and a sudden vanishing of the toiling smoke, a white flame leaps among the light wood, and darts through the great pile, and comes licking round the forestick with live tongues, and with a crackle and a roar goes sweeping and waving through the whole chimney-front.

There should be space in a chimney for good show of flame. The little deep-seated French fireplaces, where only one or two small sticks of a foot in length smoulder away, offer nothing generous to the eye. A "cut" of two feet, and an opening of three to four, is the least that can revive the pageantry of an old-time flame, and the traditions of that fireside which gives its gleam and play to the winter nights of old tales and poems. Five and six feet of width belonged to the old tavern fires of New England, around which village gossips made circle, and where three or four flip-irons might find a tempting redness. As for the chimney-corner which admitted a child or two, or some crunched-up figure of a dame, with pipe or knitting, within shelter of the jambs, it involved an amplitude of fireplace of which there are only scattered relics.

I can recall such a one in an old lumbering house of a seaport town of New England. It was below stairs in a sort of basement that had its eyelets of windows looking out upon a bold stretch of harbor, where coasters and fishing-smacks lay at anchor. Not used, save on great days (for the novelties of narrowed fires and black cooking-stoves had crept in above stairs); the cobwebs hung their tracery from the beams; the old roasting-jack that stood athwart the chimney opening was rusted; the great iron crane bore no burden of kettles; the hearth with its spent brands and its heap of moistened ashes slumbered for weeks together; but the fire-dogs were in place, and a wilderness of cupboards to the right and to the left still piqued curiosity. I can remember how a company of us roistering youngsters equipped those cupboards one day on the sly; a brown paper parcel (it may have been salt or sausages), a couplet of bottles of small beer in another corner, a relay of potatoes, a loaf of baker's bread, a pound or two of box raisins for dessert, a dozen or more of nice baking apples, and, grandest of all, a fat fowl ready for the spit; but no spit had we, — such effeminacy was discarded; we oiled the bearings of the rusty roasting-jack, and presently, by the light of a great roaring blaze, set the prized fowl a-twirling. And what a savory odor exuded as the flesh began to brown, and what a basting we gave it with the drip into the extemporized sauce-pan which we had planted below upon the heaped-up firebrands! There was some hot drink, too, simmering away in the corner, — a sort of mulled beer, and a row of toasting apples, and a score of potatoes coming to a mealy ripeness under the hot ashes. At last the banquet was spread out upon an oaken cross-legged table as old as the fireplace; and we rioted upon the spoils with a gusto that I think none of us have felt over the grandest suppers since. The huge chimney and the roaring mass of white flame, and the self-helping, were marvellous appetizers.

I am inclined to think that the subject of chimneys ought to have a literature of its own, — ending in smoke, very likely; but the trailing blue pennant over a house-top is a symbol of domesticity, and a token of civilization. A savage fire and a heathen fire squanders its color in the woods, or its smoke finds vent from some gross aperture of a cavern or hut, and is not borne up by that ascending current which belongs only to the chimney flue, and which carries its little fireside waifs and wreaths of blue writing upon the sky. The fat thrushes of the Roman times were cooked under difficulties; Horace has his plaint about smarting eyes in a smoky hostelry, and it is quite certain that Tiberius never had a good draft to his fire on any winter's day in his best palace. Herculaneum shows no chimneys, and the marble houses of Augustus, when they had fires in them, must have given ooze to the smoke out of doorways, or some crude scuttle in the roof. Who can tell what the Delias and Lucretias of those times may have suffered when the wood was wet, and the *paterfamilias* sour? But it must be mentioned, in justice to provident husbands of that day, that amiable ones took the precaution to give their fuel a previous baking, so that it might consume away with as little smoke as possible. For all this, the *atrium* (as its name implies) must have been a terrible murky place, and Vitruvius cautions against too much carved work, which will gather soot, and require infinite labor for the cleaning.

At what date a true chimney first carried its streamer of blue above the house-tops, is a vexed question, — certainly not much before the fourteenth century, if so early as then. The Venetian chroniclers are sturdy advocates of the Venetian claim to their first adoption ; and, if we may believe the most zealous among them, old Dandolo may have been regaled with the sight of chimney-tops pouring out their wavelets of smoke, when he sailed back from his brave conquest of the great city of the Dardanelles. The representative word for chimneys — *Caminus* — does certainly appear in the chronicles of a time long anterior to this event. But when did chimneys cease to mean a mere vent for the smoke, and when did they begin to mean a piled-up flue that should give draft and token of something like a fireside below?

In a chronicle of the year 1347[1] there is indeed mention of a great earthquake, and further mention (only casual, and so more fitting for testimony) that a great many chimneys were toppled over by it. This, certainly, is positive; for by no stretch of imagination can we conceive of a mere hole in the wall or roof being toppled over. Hereabout, then, Mr. Beckmann, in his history of inventions (which is only so full as to pique, and no way satisfy), places the start-point of chimneys proper.

But suppose — say the sturdy Venetian antiquarians of our day — that an earthquake of a century previous was not powerful enough to stir the chimneys, or suppose the mortar was better, or suppose the chronicler was not so observant of so homely facts? I leave the doubt and the date in a curl of smoke — from my pipe.

Quite certain it is, however, that many of our traditional notions of old English firesides are less smoky than they should be. Through those early centuries, England was a long way behind Italy in

---

[1] A much earlier date of similar occurrence is given by Filiasi (*Veneti Primi et Secondi*), who claims chimneys for Venetians from " time immemorial."

the fashion of her houses and her cookery. If Jessica had no chimney-corner to nestle in, it is more than probable that her flax-haired contemporary in London had none. King Alfred never watched the cooking of the cakes (of the neatherd's wife) upon anything like what we should call a hearth; and the chances are ten to one that the good Saxon king suffered from smarting eyes in that season of his moralizing. Henry Beauclerc and the enterprising Matilda (who crossed the river at Oxford on the ice, all clad in white, to escape from the renegade Stephen), never knew the comforts of a good, cosy fireside. It is doubtful even if Scott, ordinarily so correct in matters of history, has not stretched a point in arranging so comfortable a chimney-corner in the house of Cedric the Saxon, where Isaac the Jew and the disinherited knight hobnobbed together, on their way to the great tournament of Ashby de la Zouche.

If the Saxon host had a tolerably good chimney in those days, at either end of the hall, he had what few of his fellow-landholders in England had, whether Saxon or Norman. But with the glamour of that rich story of Ivanhoe floating before me, such punctilious historic inquiry seems only impertinent. I shall never cease to believe (whatever Beckmann may say) in a good, generous fireplace, at the foot and at the head of the great low hall of the Saxon franklin; I shall never cease to believe in the cringing figure of Isaac of York, screening himself as he best may in the shadow of the jambs; I shall never cease to believe in the thin, earnest face of Ivanhoe, glowing in the light of that fireside, and stealing glances across the long line of table to the queenly and ice-cold Rowena; I shall never cease to believe in the fire-play glimmering over those old oaken rafters of Cedric the Saxon, and lighting up the swart visage of Brian de Bois-Guilbert, any more than I shall cease to believe in the next day's journey toward the tournament, or in the slouching giant in black armor who won the battle, or in the half-veiled bosom of the pretty Rebecca, or in any minutest item of that grand old story of Ivanhoe.

The real truth was, I suspect, that in Cœur de Lion's day, most hall fires were made upon a rude stone hearth in the centre of the apartment, and that the smoke found its way out of vent-holes at either end of the roof.

If the men of Venice were the first to construct modern chimneys, it is quite certain that the modern men of Venice have not kept pace with the progress of the art; for I doubt if, on the score of drafts, a more villainously constructed set of chimneys is to be found in the world than in that city of gondolas. Smoking fires are not rare anywhere in Italy; but in Venice, — whether by reason of the blasts that sweep down from the Vicentine Mountains, or the eddies of wind in the narrow streetways, — a freely drawing chimney is most rare. The writer can never forget, and will not forbear to tell, a certain illustrative experience of his own, within a quiet little house, which was seated in a garden upon the banks of the Grand Canal.

Through all the autumn months I had eyed, suspiciously, certain sooty stains, which stretched from the fireplace up the frescoed wall; yet my landlord — a *débonnair* little Frenchman, who had come thither in the trail of the Marshal Marmont as his *major-domo*, and who had inherited most of that old sinner's household goods — assured me that the chimney drew "charmingly." It was indeed a coquettish-looking affair for a fireplace, with a quantity of brazen trappings, and polished steel grate; and upon a sour November day, — far earlier than most people in that region think of the luxury of a fire, — I placed in it a little fagot of sticks that had grown upon some one of the capes of Istria, and lighting it coyly, threw myself back in my chair for an enjoyment of that home-like cheer which a rollicking blaze upon the hearth is apt to breed in a ruminative man.

There came a blaze to be sure; but with it such a persistent, intermittent outpouring of smoke, as half-blinded and wholly maddened me. I summoned the Frenchman, who came in his black velvet cap with gold tassel, and posed theatrically before the chimney. He had never, — never seen the like of it, *parole d'honneur;* he was all astonishment; he thought the wood must be wet; and, again, thought there was too much wood; two sticks, three sticks were quite enough; wood was *excessivement* dear (in which he was quite right); besides which, there must be a draft through the room, — such a door must be opened, — a little crack in a window as well, and he explained to me kindly what the action of fire was in promoting currents of air (with a wealth of pretty gesticulation), and how new supplies of air were needed, and how a Russian princess had occupied the same apartments, and had been "ravished" by the little fireplace and its brazen adornments.

To all which I listened in a dazed way, half-blinded still by the smoke, and watching through the murk the swaying tassel of my landlord's cap as he grew earnest in exposition. I yielded mechanically to his various suggestions; the quantity of wood was reduced to the Venetian standard; the door was set ajar; the window had its scapement;

the new currents were set a-flow; but the chimney maintained its obstinacy. If there was less smoke, it was only because there was less of fire; if there was less of murkiness about the walls of the little salon, it was because the keen November winds from off the lagoon were drifting in. I tried faithfully to live at Rome like the Romans, and to yield to the objurgations of my tasselled friend, and believe that all was *parfaitement* clear. A week or more of this sort of acclimatization only made my eyes the sorer, and my temper the sourer, until the Yankee in me declared itself for revolution.

I summoned anew my tasselled friend, and informed him that, whatever the yielding Russian princess might have thought, my own notion was, that his chimney was good for nothing. I insisted upon thorough investigation. So we called up a workman from an adjoining court, and down came the brazen trappings, disclosing a great chimney-mouth deeper than the fireplace itself. I ordered up brick and mortar, and set the mason at work to build up the chimney-back anew. Both mason and landlord were astounded by my pretentions. Yet both carried out my directions with very much the same interest, I thought, with which they would have humored the fancies of a lunatic. The throat was narrowed by eight inches or more; the frontal blazonry of metal was brought down to meet this new advance of the masonry behind, and when all was complete, and the work fairly dried, I summoned my tasselled friend to see the result. We lighted a great fagot and thrust it in; there was a crackle and a blaze, and a succession of pouring flame that went roaring up the new throat of the chimney, carrying every twirling jet of smoke or vapor, — so complete a success, in short, that even the *major-domo* clapped his hands and cried, "*C'est magnifique!*"

I never sat by a fireside that was better proof against erring jets of smoke, — never knew a haler and cheerier roar through any chimney-throat than in that Yankee-improved one of Venice. The *major-domo* brought his friends to look at it and to wonder. I doubt if the *major-domo* has ceased wondering yet. I am credibly informed that he exhibits it with pride to curious lodgers as an extraordinary chimney, — a chimney *à l'Américain*. It is questionable if there be a better chimney in Venice to-day; and I trust the egotism will be pardoned if I say that I regard it as the solitary triumph of a short and not eminently lucrative consular career, in that city of boats and palaces.

If the Venetians of modern times are not apt in the construction of a good chimney for draft, they are certainly not without abundant architectural fancies in the construction of chimney-tops. In no city are they more various, more quaint, or more picturesque; nor is this an unworthy direction wherein architectural ability may disport itself. It is the crowning finial of the house; the campanile, and ventilator, and cupola, in comparison with it, are mere adventitious excrescences. These tell nothing of the fireside, and may be packed with equal significance upon a stable, or a Tammany Hall, or a State capitol. But the chimney — most of all, a group of chimneys — tells a story of the family, and of the chimney-corner, and of smoking breakfasts, and of the prattle of little ones. It is the complement of every true home. Why not give it grace? Expensive materials are no way essential; wonders can be done with ordinary brick by adroit juxtaposition; and if those of different colors are selected, very charming effects may be wrought out, even in the smallest cottage chimneys. Those who have seen the brick chimneys upon Hampton Court and Eton College will have a hint of what I would suggest. The earthen ornamental chimney-pots which were in favor a few years ago are excessively cockneyish, and carry no flavor of that sturdy hospitality which a home-like chimney should show by its mass and its solidity. In the country-house there is of course more range for such over-roof demonstration than in the town, where narrowness of space, and narrower conventionalisms, will compel uniform appearance; or, what is worse, compel a resort to those metallic whirligigs which may carry away smoke, indeed, but carry away at the same time all dignity from the hearth-stone. No hearth-stones in fact belong to them, since they are only the patent indicators and adjuncts of some patent device for packing all heat appliances into some kindred metallic abomination of a stove.

The honest wood-fire should be upon the same level with the floor, and diffuse its glow all abroad. Hence even that economic broad-cheeked device of the Franklin-stove lacks at least one of the proper requirements. There is a line of murky blackness between hearth and floor, which irks terribly a man who is used to plant himself of a winter's morning upon a good, solid hearth-stone. There is a mending of the matter indeed, which has its consolations; the iron bottom may be discarded, and the superstructure dropped directly upon the hearth, thus securing the economies of the great economizer's plan, and giving the regalement of a clean and clear level for the fire. I have put this method in practice for a good many years now, with a very serene satisfaction.

I doubt if the people of any Southern or semi-tropical countries know the fullness and richness which, for a Northerner, lie crowded in that word *FIRESIDE*. The Italian shortcomings I have hinted at; and where wood is marketed by the pound, and an armful is a godsend for a week, there is reason for shortcoming. But on the Albanian hills, where fagots of ripe alder are not worth a king's ransom, the blundering people have no keen relish for a great blaze and its domestic accompaniments; and within stone's throw of abounding wood upon the Apennines, you shall see old women in the mountain houses, besetting a little meagre earthen brazier of fuming charcoal. Happily the loose doors and windows spare them the pains of poisoning.

In our own country, as you get southward of the Potomac, you begin to see the chimneys built up outside the houses, giving them a raw and inhospitable look. Even in well-appointed homesteads, where all other cheer used to abound, the fires depended upon such chance supplies of green, sappy wood, and were so lost in the depths of monstrous broad-throated chimneys, as to belie all the New England traditions of fireside comfort.

Without being much versed in the culinary art, it does seem to me that the fullest accomplishment in that line must belong to a great open hearth. Is it conceivable that the tight, closed, prison-like, black ranges of our modern kitchens can put a plump turkey to that kindly, blistered, chocolate-colored browning, which used to belong to that coveted edible in the boy-days of broad fires and toasted drum-sticks? Are there ashes about wherein a boy may slip a pig's tail, wrapped in tissue-paper, and achieve that other roasting triumph? Any broad plateau of ruby coals whereon the old gridiron, with its little runlets for the juices, may be posed, preparatory to the wallop on it of a tender porter-house steak? All the time, too, a *pot au feu*, lovely with a faint blush of onion, may be singing its song in the corner of the great fireplace; and presently the artist may come (in paper cap, if he lives in France), and toss an omelet out of his bright, long-handled sauce-pan, in a twinkling, from over the streaming blaze.

Is it true that the dismal range is capable of these things?

There be quite other meats, too, which — seems to me — always got their finest and rarest taste in the glow of a great roaring January fire, when the hearth was swept and the curtains drawn.

What feasts there were to be sure in those winter nights, with Mr. De Foe and Miss Porter and all the rest, for furnishers and providers! What a choice morsel was that marvellous story of Sindbad the Sailor, and how old Ali Baba and the Forty Thieves regaled us! From my soul I pity those later born youth, who come to their first knowledge and taste of such delicacies under the toasting of an anthracite stove, or a patent register! Even as we listened in those old times, with eyes intent upon the blaze, every sudden flicker was a watchfire on the Scottish mountains, every tumble of a brand was a flash of the fierce Kirkpatrick's claymore, and a sudden burst of sparks was a flight of arrows from the English bowmen. As for Crusoe, he made his voyage, and suffered wreck, and saved his stores, and dug his cavern, — all under the forestick, where our eyes rested. Some oysters (in the shell), simmering upon the coals, and presently opening with a gape, were the Friday victims of some cannibal folk, and (horror of horrors!) we shortly turned cannibals ourselves, and laughed away all thought of indigestion.

Or, if we of larger growth, knuckled down ourselves to the dog's-eared volumes, with elbows on the table, every unusual flash of light from the waving fire was a burst of some magic vase in the pages of the Arabian Nights, and every rustle in the embers seemed the stealthy tread of some one of the Forty Thieves. Even the slightest crackle on the hearth offered somehow a grateful symphony with the rare tone of those grand old stories.

Well, we shall never read them again as we read them once. Adieu, sweet Helen Mar! Adieu, Amanda! Adieu, old Scheherazade!

The decorators with all their arts and all their vermilion and gold can never match the blaze from the Fireside. I think we might well spare our spendings in other directions for the sake of keeping alive this flame — so full of traditional charm — so full of joyousness and cheer.

It is the wisest, fullest, fittest, richest of all the decorative adjuncts of a home room. It redeems poverty of equipment; it gilds the plainest furniture; it sheds cheerful illumination over the scantest of floors; it kindles the best tints on soberest of ceilings; it steals with its warm reflections the chillness from the deadest of carven images; it puts a roseate flush (that is more than Capo-Monti, or Dresden finish) on simplest cottage crockery; it gilds the backs of homeliest books — making them each one, a Roger Payne in binding; it deepens by contrast the dark embayed corners of your room, so that Rembrandtish effects are your companions; it wakens fairy glimpses into fairy realms of shadow; it sets astir depths of sentiment — for which no man ever is the worse — as it brings into view under its ruddy glow, portraits of lost ones upon your walls — eyes long closed are touched with a tenderer light —

> "There is no Fireside howsoe'er defended
> But has one vacant chair."

Is it a phantom fire, that I see once again? A hearth all swept; gigantic brazen fire-dogs, with minarets and quadrant balustrade sweeping round half the hearth, with minarets and balustrade shining like gold; a great back-log, half spent, and checkered with irregular squares of red coal; a hickory fore-stick round which the white fingers of flame play and dance; a broad red glow of firelight on the ceiling; a sparkle of brightness on the hyacinth glasses upon the ledge of the windows, waiting to-morrow's sun; a diffused, mellow, wavering play of light over hearth-rug and carpet, out to the dim wilderness where the chairs rise like trees planted in fours; a dog, half in shadow and half in light, who if one says "Watch!" (sharply) lifts his head, and tracks the voice, and comes out of the dimness to lick the hand of the caller; a round table, comfortably near the hearth, whereon a tall astral lamp throws down a softened glow of light; a gray-haired man, with spectacles on nose, who reads: "*For now we see through a glass darkly —*"; a lady in white cap, who listens, and as she listens, shifts the needles in some boyish wrap of winter; a girl with golden ringlets, in the which her fingers are weaving a vision, as she looks meditatively at the glowing embers; a curly-pated boy, with face in shadow, whose hand is on the dog "Watch" —

Phantoms, — phantoms all!

Highways and Parks.

NARROW streets make long death-rolls; but narrowness is not a constant quantity. It is a thing of conditions. If New Yorkers persist in building such towers as flank the corners of Beekman Street and Nassau, they will presently reduce either of those streets to a condition which it would delight a Sanitarian to ventilate — by discussion. But there must be not only spaces for sun and air; there must also be in the wider openings, with which an orderly civilization should cleave the streets — foliage. Vigorous trees are great disinfectants. Their lively laboratories appropriate what is bad, and set free what is good.

Indeed, an ideal city — when we have one — from a sanitary point of view, should have its little nucleus of business quarters upon a bay, or a river, or a great thoroughfare — as the case might be; and this business nucleus crystallizing there under the compression of an outlying circle of green, jealously guarded, would project its rays, or avenues of traffic athwart this circle; and these avenues of traffic, by their accretions of lesser and lighter business, would demand zebra-like cross-bars of space and greenness and foliage, to be flanked with files of houses — in such sort that a man could not go to his business without sight of trees, or a chance to put his foot to the live earth; while all schools and courts and hospitals should have their setting of green.

This sounds fanciful; but it is not fanciful at all, and is only another way of setting forth that interspacing of greenness and air with brick and stone, which the best sanitary regimen is trying to bring about at prodigious costs, in nearly all the old cities of the world.

The only question is, how much of this curative of green leaves, which are heaven appointed — "*for the healing of the nations*" — shall be thrust in amid the crowded alleys of cities, and wedge them open to light and air.

A good array of figures well placed and well footed, will force us to the belief that such, and such another disposition of ground, or buildings, or trees, is contributory to public health; but all the figures of the best statisticians alive will not convince us that this or that disposition of natural objects is beautiful, and by right, should be a delight to us always. This must come of an art-sense which is shapen by education. And I have faith that there will come a time — not this year, nor in ten years — but some day, when the data for judgment in matters of art will be as fixed as are now the data for judgment in matters of engineering. In that good day coming we shall have bridges not only scientifically constructed, but at every point æsthetically good; and the rarest and fullest obedience to all the laws of scientific construction in bridge, or court, or spire, will carry about it a delightful harmony with all the subtlest rulings of grace.

Meantime, I want to lay stress upon the fact that all such treatment of ground as we shall consider involves an artistic eye and artistic handling; and so is brought under the domain of Art. It is not a problem in engineering that may be worked out by laws laid down in the books.

Take, for instance, the trail of a park road; it involves, indeed, good engineering; but it involves more. There must be grace, there must be winningness in every line; there must be dalliance with the low declivities, there must be easy and scarce discoverable gain upon the altitudes which are surmounted only for the charms of outlook they offer.

The engineer aims at easy traffic, and the most economic methods of securing it. But such considerations do not belong to a scheme of park roads, where the aim is leisurely recreation. Again, the little, meaningless curves, and sharp, sudden turns which may come of too close an economy are so many impertinences and interferences with that large enjoyment and regalement which park roads ought to offer in all their lines.

Least of all should there be any palpable and arrogant show of engineering triumphs; a park drive should conquer difficulties of surface so subtly and gracefully as to leave no traces of the struggle; and that achievement is best of all which makes the resulting street or drive seem — much as possible — to have been laid down along some happy accident of surface — evolved by the processes of nature, with no ambitious scars of quarryman, or miner, challenging the eye. The painter whose manner is forever calling attention to his *technique*, and the thrusts of his brush, never coins such triumphs as the one who makes you forget the details of his workmanship, in the charm with which he enthralls you.

Again, recognition of the art quality, which should belong to all judicious treatment of public grounds, will put at a discount much of that bustling, business-like, pushing, common-council capacity, which attacks the question of park drives, or bridges, or fountains, or monuments, very much as it would attack a dinner of beef and cabbage, and with a feeling that a good healthy stomach — not much brain being needed — would digest it all very easily. Fortunately there are common-council men who have taste as well as energy, as there are engineers who unite art-feeling to skill; I have heard even of aldermen thus exceptionally endowed. For this we should be grateful.

It is certain, however, that we shall never come to the measure of best work on public ground, whether as parks or highways, or village commons, until we come to full recognition of the fact that there is an art quality in all good works of the sort which by right furtherance will make of our roads, and greens, and school-yards great helpers in the ways of refinement and of civilization.

A well-cared for, and well-ordered highway may in itself take on park-like attributes, and carry with it into the midst of many a small town all that rural flavor and much of the adornment which we associate with parks. I need do no more than allude to those old-fashioned New-England towns — lying here and there in the laps of the hills — into which you enter by green ways, under boughs of elm trees, or of maple, and find the houses with neat door-yards

before them, flanking a great, broadened highway,—
so broad that the wheel tracks have gone on either
side, leaving a green common between, shaded by
ponderous-limbed trees. Here are all the park elements which will suffice for years of growth; and
which, if there be neatness and order, the most
skilled of gardeners cannot touch without blundering into niceties that will weaken, instead of strength-
ening general effect.

The trim barriers or railings — all the worse
if they are ambitious ones of iron — which an
ugly conventionalism will sometimes plant around
such middle part of a great broadened highway
is only belittling — neither carrying grace of its
own, nor lending grace; and if all the dwellers
about such rural common could have the healthy
hardihood to tear away their own enclosures —
fronting them, and flanking them, and boxing them
in, for which, in nine cases in ten, there is no more
real service than for lamps in the daytime — the
whole centre of the township could be straightway
converted into a park, with all its best appointments of shrub and tree. I understand perfectly
that there may be private walks — gardens in the
rear, which must have their barriers and screens;
but in the great majority of instances — all that
space, ordinarily boxed into what is called a front

door-yard in rural villages might be opened to the road, with great gain, pecuniary and æsthetic, to all concerned.

Though in many of our public parks we have pushed matters to a very high stage of artistic development, yet as respects our country roads and highways we still border very closely upon savagery. It is not the road-bed proper, which is so bad — though that is many times execrable; but it is its environment of mud-pits, of bald boulders, of broken banks, which — wherever easiest digging prompted — are made cavernous so as to undermine adjoining walls — all rubbish from neighboring farm lands being dumped there at intervals; and so soon as the kindly vines and brushwood accomplish a little leafy screen for such barbarities, there comes an awful "slicking up" by destruction of all these kindly fig-leaves which nature had put upon the unclean doings of selectmen or other road-masters, leaving frightful array of stubs and ash-heaps, and blackened stones, and despoiled and struggling brakes and briars. There is mission work needed here, for which I fear the architectural elegancies of city parks do not preach the best sermons. And country folk who go to gape and wonder are as little impressed with a saving conviction as a heathen and thorough reprobate would be, by the exaltation of Keble's "Christian Year."

I know nothing which would be more provocative of that rural grace of heart which public parks are supposed to nourish, than a new, and lively, and persistent attention to the comeliness of our waysides; nor is there any good reason why every country road leading up to large or small interior towns, should not by its invitingness of aspect, and unpretending and uncostly rural graces, make an everyday trail of æsthetic teaching. More than any parks, I think, even by many cities and towns which begin to talk of them, there is needed attention to their suburban highways. They should be laid out — not as every land-owner scheming for long frontages may desire — not as every city engineer intent upon nothing but UTTER grading may propose — but as the largest features of the land, and most intelligent estimate of future growth may demand.

Most of these roads will diverge to other and adjoining townships; so there will be radiation of lines, which in the outskirts will give little triangular spaces to be held in reserve for parklets, for a public building, a clock-tower, a fountain, a monument. Then, naturally, there come about joinings of these outgoing divergent highways by lesser cross-roads — cut through mostly as easy traffic may decide; and in many a growing town — just becoming emulous of parks — such cross-roads by a doubling or quadrupling of their breadth, and judicious planting would make a great, irregular, encircling park-like belt of space and of greenness — accessible from all points — a delight to young and old, and by so much better than a formal park, because it is married with all the economies of their daily life and traffic.

Again, in such transfiguration of high-roads to larger ends, it is to be considered that the widening process may touch upon some unsightly and comparatively worthless localities — as morasses, bits of cliff — which may be wrought into the scheme, by special enlargement thereabout of its boundaries, and the morass be changed into a limpid pool of water, and the cliff taught to wear its tresses of vines and its plumes of foliage.

It is amazing what skill and courage and patience may do with unsightly things. I have seen a broad mud-flat in the very eye of a town — left bare at every tide — which, by the deposit of judicious dredgings upon wattled mattresses of brush, came to show ultimately an irregular peninsula of raised earth, with thrifty-growing wooded-walks upon it, and the ripples breaking cleanly and sparklingly against its borders at every stage of the tide.

Another instance of the conversion of an area of unmitigated ugliness to park-like uses and beauty, is so notable that I venture to give a detail or two of conditions and results. I allude to the *Buttes de Chaumont* in Paris. It is or was high ground, once called Mont-Faucon, to the northeast of the city, over Belleville way. It was a place for executions a long time, and men used to hang in chains there upon the bald, bare top of the hill: then quarries were worked there, making unsightly pits, and leaving raw scars of yellow rock: all the offal of the city, for years and years, was taken thither, and thence came the first makings of poudrette for farm uses — the screenings, and sunnings, and manipulations to that end, all taking place on this bald, treeless, scathed hill of gibbets. Thieves burrowed in the holes which quarrymen had left, and the lower pits were rank with the accumulated ooze from the offal and foul industries of the locality.

It was Mr. Haussmann, the intrepid master of improvements under Louis Napoleon, who took this in hand for a cleansing, or if it might be — some park-like decoration. The result anybody can see who will go out to Villette — a region of the *Communistes* — and not otherwise inviting. The lower levels at the foot of the old quarry are all drowned in a beautiful limpid lake, which is fed by a rivulet flowing down from unseen sources in the rock. The bald flank of the hill is covered with lawn, and scattered coppices. Upon a shelf of the high ground a cottage restaurant is embowered in trees; the old scarred cliffs are lichened over or covered with ivies; a light wire bridge swings from height to height above the bed of the lake; and by this you may pass over to the craggy tower of rock which the quarrymen had left isolated, and from whose top you may look sheer down upon the water at its base, upon the groups of children loitering along the paths, upon the emerald green of the meadow which flanks the pool and that stretches out shimmering in the sun to a near wall of foliage, over which appear against the haze, or the blue of the sky, the roofs and towers and domes of that wonderful city of Paris.

Of course all this cost a great deal of money; but the enhanced taxable value of surrounding property goes very far toward covering costs, if it does not before now completely do so. At the same time a waste of ground, unsightly and polluting, has been converted into a blooming garden, whose civilizing influences are felt in all that region — neatness and order coming at last to stand for something of positive value, and the children of the neighborhood — by loitering in these trim walks, and by contact with others there, and the pretty emulation growing out of it—becoming more cleanly and comely, yielding thus, in habit, insensibly to their new surroundings.

I was speaking a little way back about schoolyards and hospital-yards in connection with our out-of-door æsthetics. And why not?

In larger cities, it is true, schools are brought squarely to the street edge, and by preposterous and slavish imitation, in far too many of our smaller cities; but in country towns there is verge and space, for the most part overgrown with dreary turf, or may be, by exceptional zeal for ornament carrying two or three pyramidal evergreens, stiff as grenadiers, of whose names and habits very likely both teachers and pupils are ignorant. Well, why not bring this space under a sort of park endowment, with trees, or shrubs, or flowers, or—if area permit—all of these together; not as so much dead rubbish to be planted and never looked after, but to be watched, to be labelled, to represent special *genera*, to be noted and classified, to become a part of the paraphernalia of the school as much as the physical geography-maps, or the globe, or the air-pump—if they have one?

Would not children come kindly to such out-of-door lessons, and to such practical knowledge as would always bestand them well? And from such object lessons, might we not hope, in due course, for a crop of burgesses who would look after highways with some intelligent sense of their best equipment and a zeal quickened by knowledge?

If I join jail-yards to this mention of school enclosures, and what may be helpfully done with them, do not count me among those sentimental folk who would force cologne and confits upon criminals, and follow them up with a bevy of women sympathizers: I have, what seems to me, a wholesome belief that a bad man should carry with him everywhere a stinging sense of his badness — not to be hoisted out of him by eleemosynary sweets. But I have also such faith in the right and loving treatment of nature's furnishings of flower and tree, as to believe that the right adjustment of them before the eyes of the most criminal will, in due time, engage the mind and possess it, to the exclusion of a good many of the devil's artifices. A bald, sandy court, or one reeking with mud-pools and garbage, would set all the rogue's blood in a body to the boil — when the same court turfed, and garnished with the fleecy shadows of playing foliage or flecks of bloom, would wean from deviltries as much as a good sermon — and a good deal more than an average one.

But whatever may be true of the criminal class and of the possible influence of those surroundings which show the most winning side of nature, there can be no doubt of this influence in the case of those weak-minded and distraught ones who people our retreats for the insane.

To these, the order, the repose, the graceful contours, the restful shade, the burst of a thousand flowers, the dash and sparkle of water, bring a self-forgetting which is a gain and a delight. There is danger of falling into a strain here which will sound like mere sentiment with no substantive record at its back; but such fact substance is not wanting. A veteran superintendent of one of our largest institutions for the insane in the country, said to me, "I know nothing of all curatives within our reach which, in case of deflection of the mental forces, will so soothe and catch and hold the distrained mind — so allure and so cheat it into escape from its own vagaries as well-ordered and attractive park-gardening."

Passing now from a consideration of these lesser holdings of public lands, which may wisely be made subject of æsthetic treatment, I come to a mention of those great reservations of territory — such as the Yosemite Valley and the country of the Yellowstone — which have come to be called National Parks. These in their mountain lines and their stupendous fissures carry their own blazon of work wonderfully done; and æstheticism has no call in their presence, save to admire and let severely alone. Government duty in respect of both is summed up in a phrase — *Make access easy and guard from despoilment.*

Among State reservations (or proposed reservations) for so-called park purposes, is to be noted the much-mooted one — in late years — of a certain prescribed area along the banks of Niagara River. It is understood that action in regard to the latter is stayed (or at least impeded) by the opinion of some expert that the area prescribed in the initiatory legislation is not sufficiently extended. It is much to be regretted that a scheme which so commends itself to every man up to the level of appreciating nature's wonders, should be impeded by trivialities or by antagonisms in the commission having the work in charge. It is to be hoped, however, that when these are laid, and the scheme meets fulfilment, that the Niagara region will escape the impertinences of fine gardening, or of ambitious architectural display; and that the commission will recognize the fact that the grandest park achievement needed — will be to give free way to the world, through stately alleys of wood, to unencumbered banks, and open sight of the great spectacle of waters.

The Adirondacks have been made subject of legislation more positive in its issues; but with respect to this reservation it is understood that very prompt action is now necessary to guard against spoliation; and broad trails should be laid bare—where they will be least disfiguring—to guard against the sweep of forest fires: beyond this, and the enforcement of rigid forestry laws, the Adirondack Park will "run itself."

Other States might well follow the example of New York in the matter of such reservations of wild land; Georgia has a wealth of forest and waterfalls in its north-western region; North Carolina in its mountain valleys; Virginia along the Blue Ridge; Pennsylvania in the Alleghanies, and New Hampshire and Maine among their lakes and mountains which are worthy of legislative guardianship.

The belief is, I think, now fully established—that the destruction of forests and consequent denudation of the hill lands stifles the mountain springs, and puts in peril our water supply. New England is feeling a scantiness on this score, more and more stringently every year. It is evident that legislation must speedily take cognizance of this threatened peril; and how better, than by acquiring title—if such is not already held by the State—to a great forest range, and demonstrating and illustrating there the best conditions for its conservation?

I next come to speak of what we currently call

city parks — of their beginnings and of their methods of growth, and of how some of those methods may perhaps be mended.

It is not often that a city or town goes openly into market, like another buyer — for park land; the scheme gets started quietly and evolves through a world of cautious manœuvres; or the gift of a dead man or living gives consequence and a start-point; or there is some modification of large surface undertaken for sanitary purposes, which as it progresses suggests and invites such artistic treatment as results in a great pleasure ground; but whenever and wherever it becomes a thing of city purchase for declared purpose of park-making, there should be full report by a legally appointed commission on all available sites, that choice may be open, and have the weight of the popular authority on its side. Any such project which is brought about by chicane or underworking will be handicapped from the start by a certain amount of quiet antagonism, and certainly lack that spontaneity of support which gives best results.

Again, whatever a town does in this way, it should do with full-heartedness and an open hand. Appeals to private munificence in such a work are inglorious: a town that is not ready to be taxed for a public park which offers pleasure ground for the convenience of all, is not ready for that enjoyment and that zealous appreciation which alone gives such project its best conservation.

I have no great faith in the park tendencies of a town which has not already done the most it can do in the proper and orderly equipment of its suburban highways, its school enclosures, its little outlying angles of waste ground. The attention given there can alone ripen the æsthetic spirit which may later take larger bloom in the glories of a park.

There can be no doubt of the fact that no outlying reach of park land, however treated, can ever compensate for the lack of open squares or gardens within a city, and easily accessible.

For the solid enjoyment of the masses and their guidance in all rural proclivities, the Bois de Boulogne without Paris, will not compare for a moment with the Monceaux and the Batignolles, and the gardens of the Luxembourg, and the Tuileries.

It might almost be said that a city which did not scrupulously regard and care for its lesser waste places deserved no park privileges at all. And these lesser breathing places of a city should have each their special treatment, guided — not by gardeners who gloat over riotous splendors -- but by considerate regard for the habits and needs of each neighborhood. Thus, near to great houses whose occupants have large range for their pleasures, treatment might well be of the severest — limited to trees and lawn surfaces; in neighborhoods where the families of workingmen congregate, there should be parterres of flowers — space for child play — and whatever within æsthetic limits will contribute most to their pleasures.

I remark, again, a strong American tendency in late years to excessive over-ornamentation of ground in public places — convoluted whirls of surface which carry no meaning in them — excessive martinetism in trimmings of walk and turf — legions of foliage plants, that fatigue one with their great reaches of tawdry color.

I suppose it to be the efflorescence of that pseudo-æstheticism which has had other outcome in Sunflowers, and *Dude-ism*, and crazy quilts, and crushed strawberry tints. This *yellowed* demonstrativeness is all the more afflictive when it is associated with utter neglect of the commoner laws of neatness and fitness, which must everywhere be the bases of all the higher reaches of æsthetic endeavor. There are Western cities, for instance, which with the most monstrous disregard for cleanliness or safety in the walks along their streets, yet string roods and roods of the most garish of flowers upon their closely shaven park grounds:

— just so some buxom, ill-trained damsel from the interior, will pace along city streets with a great top-gear of flaunting feathers and ribbons, all the while loftily unconscious of the cow-skin brogans in which she walks!

Extraordinarily bad things in dress, in gardening, and in literature are almost always done by those who try to do too much.

It is quite impossible to lay down laws for the proper treatment of park ground. Every city and community has its own needs; every landscape must have special interpretation of its compass and aptitudes. Everywhere and under all conditions, however, treatment must be large and liberal, and not wasted in petty prettinesses. I doubt the wisdom of large architectural investiture — in a cold climate like ours. Terraces and their accompaniments of sculpture, balustrades, and vases belong to a country where parks are a delight in winter as well as summer, and where steps are never clothed in ice.

And though I have inveighed against overstrain toward finery, do not understand me to favor a cheap simplicity. Whatever may be done, should be done thoroughly; cheap or hap-hazard work — wherever done — will declare itself sooner or later in awful ways. Good park work should teach the best methods of road-making, the best of path-making, and give to every tree and flower their completest development, and their most piquant grace.

Yet art must not glorify itself; it must be humble; it must deal reverently and lovingly with nature, and not divert her unwisely from her own sweet proclivities. Something more is needed than the Engineer, stiff with his instrumentation and his equations and his economies of line. Here are curves that want deftness, not cognizable by one fed solely on conic sections, but varying as cloud shapes vary — taking the billows of the hills into their sway — sweeping as they sweep.

Least of all can anything be worthily done in a spirit of stolid imitativeness. Gardens cannot be transferred by line — save on flattest and tamest of surfaces; and even here exigencies of soil or climate may demand their special recognition. A capital success under English skies cannot be wrought out here by simple duplication. Our suns, our flora, our surroundings forbid. The seed-core governs the rounded shape, and from American elements there must be American development: and whoso struggles contrariwise, will have as poor pay for his pains as the very fine people who would accredit a brave old British sport, by hunting tame foxes over Rhode Island potato-fields.

It used to be imagined that the nicer details of park work would not meet with the same respectful regard with us, as among European nations ; but the results in the Central Park — in the old days when kept in its best trim — have amply disproved this ; a reverent love for the beautiful things in nature, in shape of flower, and turf, and tree, is not a British trait or a French one ; it is — thank God — a trait of humanity.

And if to a kindly and protective regard for the beautiful things of Nature, can be added that sense of ownership which great public parks bestow upon idlers and half-idlers and all men, we face an aspect of the subject which goes beyond æstheticism and has politico-economic significance. In these days when the stupendous growth of fortunes touches the height and the responsibilities of old Principalities, and when corporations and monopolies, wittingly or unwittingly, are fomenting strange, wild comment — in such days I say, trees, and flowers, and walks, and lawns, at the public disposition — free as air — where every workman has equal ownership with the richest, make a capital safety-valve for the brooding unrest, and the angry, tempestuous desires, and the wide, covetous range of thought which Communism engenders.

Hereby lies a source of moral culture matching

and mating well with those other educational influences which take hold upon the more instructed. To these — the delicate beauties of park scenes — planted amidst the clangor of the town, give new readings and new comprehension of what is most subtle, and subtly true, in those poets who have put tender feeling into their descriptions of natural beauties.

To this end it is not needful that there be agreement — part to part: it is only needful that the faithful and loving treatment of public grounds do bring back that enthrallment of the feelings, and the mellifluous tones which broke on us in rare or felicitous renderings of rural scenes by the poets.

It is not requisite, I said, that repetition be complete — no more complete than an echo which, dallying with the hills, repeats the melodious chant from whose trail it sprung. I think Keble, and Herbert, and Tennyson, and Cowper all get new illustration and an educational smack from such good work on ground as we are considering. And everywhere and always that work of setting best ruralities before men, has good educational office — in piquing wonder, in kindling memories, in spurring to inquisition of nature's secrets.

Littlest things in that new realm we enter — captivate us: we see — with Wordsworth — and enjoy with him, the

"daisy's star-shaped shadow
Thrown on the surface of the naked stone."

BOUNCING indoors again, we find that narrow halls are as bad as narrow streets. There is no adornment of a hall like *breadth*. Narrowness makes waste of temper and waste of bric-a-brac. The cunningest lover of the "Lilies," of either sex wants to *spread*; and the common-sense man wants free and full room to put on his dreadnaught without rapping his knuckles against the wainscot.

The old school of builders did indeed presume that narrow houses and narrow lots compelled narrow halls; but the ingenuity of modern architects and a little bending of old habits have wrought a relaxation of this law of compulsion, and given relief from the pinch of a five-foot entrance way. Yet architectural ingenuity has very much more to accomplish still in this direction; and what it may or may not do affords fruitful topic for fuller discussion than we have space for here.

Breadth, however, can be secured, if only conventionalities be discarded, and the larger comforts kept in mind. True it may involve a little stealing from the space in adjoining rooms ; but, ordinarily, no wiser theft could be made. There should be room there for the shaking of hands and for a toss of "circulars." Mistress and maid, and a quartette of children should be able to group there, with verge and space for a last tying of the mufflers, and a last dusting of the frills.

The light may not be of the best; indeed full blaze is not desirable. At our first entrance upon a home, a little coy and doubtful peering about through a half-grayish — half-golden twilight — to lay hold upon the serenities that invite us, is better there. And such mystic glow as this may come easily through the olive-green lights of the lobby, or through some vitreous bit of wonderful opalescence — half up the stairway.

It will not be a light that will invite us to the study of minute figures ; nor is such needed in any hall. We can make out the pointing of the hands upon the old hall clock, if there be one present — (and it is a capital "Present"). We can catch the shimmer of the metal-work upon the breach of a Moorish gun, if one hangs athwart the hall; and a general, or an artist, or an archæologist, or a sportsman, or even an æsthete could not object to a good group of historic weapons. But whether there would be good light for delicate paintings, or for engravings, is quite another question; certainly no such things should be shown under conditions that would make the study of them a weariness; and this is good ruling for corridors, or halls, or libraries. What is worth seeing closely, is worth the light to see it by.

An old family portrait or two, with homely, strong lines in them, might stand well in the half-dimness of a hall, with a historic twilight upon them by day; and by night (with some kindly fixture of upper lights) taking on an aureole of welcoming smiles.

Again, an old bit of tapestry — Flemish or other — is not a bad thing for the half-dimness of a hall; not stretched straight, as if we were eager to make the very most of it, but taking easy folds into which figures of stalwart falconers, and trees, and cavaliers shall break and break out again in pretty, mystic bewilderment of change. Then this tapestry (like an arras of old) may hide things that would break upon the artistic harmonies of the hall. It may overhang and conceal a slight recess where the everyday man (though he were a Bunthorne) must keep his galoshes, and his canes, and his mackintosh, and his ulster.

And what, pray, should be under foot in our hall,

and what floor have we? That floor is best of all which by its smoothness, and evenness, and soundness, and lowness of tone as compared with all wall surfaces, makes us straightway forget what manner of floor it is. Neither our eye or thought should seek it or pursue it. If there are geometrics in it they should not be so *voyants* as to tempt us to work out their puzzles; and it is no place for perspectives, even of a cube of color. A hall mat or rug too that tells of warmth and softness is telling about the best story that it can possibly tell.

Slippery floors again (though of rarest hard woods), and floors waxed and polished to the last degree of smoothness, if they confront us in the entrance-hall, are an abomination. No man of proper sedateness, and no woman of assured domesticity but dreads setting foot upon paths that are slippery.

A good old oaken settle is not a bad thing for halls, with its sheer severities of paneled back and its sturdy plank footing; not easy to be sure; we do not want any cushioned luxuries in a hallway; it is rather a good place to receive "bores," if we must receive them at all, and an oaken settle of oldish and homely rectangularities does not tempt a long stay. The same may be said of overwrought oaken chairs with great bulges of uneasy and recreant carving; the hall is a good place for such, except they be inhibited by too palpable a non-agreement with other fixtures. But there is always this good in a hall, that it takes a "jumble" of things more justly, and carries them more easily than other rooms.

As respects disposition of apartments, it is surprising—when we undertake building (if we ever do)—how much we are governed by the conventionalities set before us by the neighbors, or by the architect; and how much we are inclined to lose sight of our own commonest comforts and everyday wants. Yet individuality may express itself as strongly, and as wisely, and as frequently in the distribution of parts, as in exterior or in furnishings. The friends we most wish to entertain will be those who will have strongest relish for the appointments which are most characteristic of our own tastes. If I go out to dine with a plain farmer, I am immensely disappointed to find his substantial corn-beef and cabbage supplanted for the day by stale *entrées* from a city caterer. We want to see people—who are worth seeing—at their truest and not at their sham best.

That interior is not interesting whose disposition of rooms and offices we can annotate by merely looking at the outside. There should be something to unfold — to allure — to charm with a pretty bewilderment. We don't want to apprehend all by exterior — as we can in so many house fronts; nor do we want to read through a man at a glance — unless he is so shallow we cannot help it; but if he have values worth computing and cherishing, we shall find them — as in well-planned houses — opening out by degrees, and keeping charm at the fullest by their delightful unexpectedness. In this matter of interior divisions the mistress of a house is, in nine cases in ten, a better judge than the master; and it would be wise to give the judgeship to one who is so apt to take it.

Whatever may be said in favor of *parqueterie* and all other pretty devices for drawing attention to the joinery of floors (where no attention should be drawn) winter weather makes one crave a wool covering that shall be grateful to the foot, and make grateful silence. Good taste and the buffalo moth have wrought together against the old-time fashion of pushing the carpeting into every angle of a room, while mats and rugs (if large enough) supply all real wants. And it is surprising and grateful to find, how — in all floor coverings, large or small — the big arabesques and flamboyancies which so delighted our grandmothers, are giving way to modester and homelier patterns. There are some purists, indeed, who tell us all floral forms should be discarded; flowers are not to be trodden on, they tell us. Well, I think such critics can know little about the glory and freedom of a dash upon a spring morning over fields that are set with blue violets and sparkle with dandelions. The more gorgeous flowers of the green-house, I will grant, are not things to be scattered carelessly; but it seems to me that on the floor of some chamber that we keep in gala dress for friends, we may well strew daisies for welcome.

In rooms more subject to usage, simplest geometric figures will be better; still more proper, perhaps, such fine confused mingling of tints as shall suggest nothing but softly dalliance with the foot, and be sure, by its negative character, to do no harm to the broidery or drapery, or other show of color which may decorate your walls.

It is a pity, I think, that we must forego in modern house construction a sight of those huge old timbers which used to go to their support in colonial times, and to stretch athwart ceilings with a show of strength that was mete for whirlwinds. Our economies have sliced them all into thin floor-beams that we take no pride in showing, and so we bury out of sight — under plaster — a constructive feature which most of any was susceptible of artistic handling. Some day, and under advances in art, I am sure the architects will lead us back to an outspoken and poetic assertion of the support which carries a roof over our heads.

Meantime, it is better every way to dress the mortar surfaces with color, rather than the ponderous plaster reliefs, which carry dust, and mean nothing. To say what that color should be would involve a book full of discussion; it should be borne in mind, however, for the benefit of whatever large or small houses we may have to deal with, that strong vertical lines of color will go to diminish apparent length of apartments, and horizontal lines to diminish apparent height. Either, or both, well adjusted, and dexterously used, may give an air of cosiness to else bare and bald interiors. Again, explosive and stunning and brilliant colors will work harm every way and everywhere; modest subjugation of tint, that will mate with furnishings, will better feed the home-feeling of those who prize it. Ambitious engarlanding of walls in fresco, may be well done; but, in that conjunction, what will you do with some quiet portrait of a grandmother? It is true that with neutral, modest tints upon the walls, you cannot push the blaze of chandeliers to such burst of brilliancy; but the ordinary home-blaze will light up fairly the friendly faces that gather at your table, and I think the glow on them will be the tenderer for a certain relief against kindly shadows.

Wainscot will have its way, and should, along the foot of some home walls; high, if rooms are high, and low, if rooms are low. It need not be costly, but as simple as tongued sheathing. In a hall of my own, I have introduced successive strips of Blackwalnut, Chestnut, Ash, Yellow and White pine, and repeated this assemblage in companies of five, all around the hall; and these are all tied to their place by a little longitudinal fillet of the dentilated Venetian moulding, which is itself relieved by a broad horizontal band of Georgia pine.

Such wainscoting may have its range of panels — each at some future day to carry such bit of home decoration as may come to the hearts or hands of those who dwell by it; or along the nursery wall, such panels, with adjustable border lines, may take on their pretty childish gear of nursery tales, their quaint lessons in stories, their legends of the flowers which grow in near woods, their picturings of the birds, which the children come to know, and so a border of lessons and delight shall stretch round the walls.

The old practise of covering all wood-work with coats of paint, is largely giving way to an exposure of natural grain, and to a more careful joinery, which has no need for cover of putty and swash of oil. The treatment has taken the name of hardwood finish; but hard-wood is by no means essential. Butternut and Chestnut are not materially harder than the coniferous woods; and our white pine, the *Strobus* of the botanists, by its very commonness has lost that appreciation for in-door finish, which I think is its due. No wood of any country stands better against all changes of temperature; and by careful selection, it may show such whirls of grain, and undulations of fibre as bring it fairly among decorative woods. Its bright tint may be subdued to any degree by a little wash of asphaltum — not in any degree obscuring the grain, nor, indeed, working so much a change of tint as an anti-dating of the color, which age would be sure to bring. But though I suggest this qualification of its newness, I would advise no varnishes; they give a distressing shine, and forbid that free contact with the air which brings swifter to all woods the mellow and delightful hues of age.

I think we never come to a full sense of what charm may lie in such simple things, until we are planted with them, and in sight of them, for days and weeks together — smitten by illness mayhap; our eyes, too weary for reading, too dazed for sleep, run over door, and wainscot,—grappling with whatever may feed daintily and consolingly that state of fevered idleness. Then the sick mind, by such door or wainscot of undisguised natural aspect, is put into refreshing company with out-of-door-nature — is set down beside great trees, and rapt into forests. It sees the actual tracery of what storms and fierce suns have wrought, and the wrenches and intricacies due to the besom of some great tempest, recorded on the panel of the door; another easy whirl of texture shows where some great limb began its growth — burdened in after-time with snows and sleet, and borne down so as to give stress all through the outer circle of tissue, and making such convolutions of woody muscle and fibre, with such show of strength and vigor, as wakens by sympathy one's own dormant energies.

How much fuller and richer all this than the dead, dull paint, with its tawny yellow of oils, and its association with some frowzy painter in a paper-cap, smelling strongly of varnish, and slipping cat-like around the premises!

Of furniture proper, I will not say much, nor is it needful. Every year, more and more of taste and of artistic consideration is brought to its construction. Though the cheapness of factory-made, florid work carries with it a certain depravation of the popular taste, the general tendency of what may be called "leading styles" is, I think, to simple severities of form. And simplicity and strength, if adapted, and grateful to use, will be sure to outlive all changes of fashion.

We all know — some of us to our cost — what an epidemic of antiquarianism has within the last ten years run over the country — dreadfully contagious, and, I think, sometimes taking on, latterly, symptoms of stark lunacy. Age, with good qualities adorning it, is certainly very much to be venerated; but I know no better reason why we should dote upon an abominably-shaped old chair, than why we should dote upon an old scoundrel of a man.

In this matter of furniture, there are those who insist upon entire keeping of the various objects — no mingling of different ages, or styles. I can understand how, — in a thoroughly appointed house, whose master loves art, and knows it, with funds for its cherishment, — entire keeping of style may properly be aimed at, and discrepancies offend. But there is no good reason why a modest householder should not avail himself of any offering chance to lay hold of a good thing, and a pretty thing, and to install it in his rooms. One object of simple good taste will not be without its lesson, even if planted amid the crookedest horrors of a flash upholstery. The extreme of propriety, and of artistic keeping in the furnishing of a home, is rather chilling than otherwise. It breeds an uncomfortable sense that our cravat will not be in keeping. What we want to warm us, is — home-like ease ; and I think it gives a measurable ease to find something undeniably out of place. Absolute and unshaken adjustment of every detail, is as fearful a thing to encounter in a house, as a man who never pronounces a word wrongly, and is always on the lookout for a bad pronunciation of yours.

Now, with respect to pictures, which every home ought to have, and may have, what shall be said? Chiefest of all, I think — don't have pictures that you can have no love for. Because all the world is agog about a new Madonna, don't have it unless you can lay your heart to it kindly. Fashion is well enough in hats, but when it sets down its foot in this domain of art, it is execrable. If the Huguenot lovers tied strange knots under trees, and the story of it brims with pretty sentiment, don't think it has exhausted all pictorial form of sentiment. Let freedom, and life, and earnest feeling go to your choosings, without any query as to our friend Mrs. Grundy. Of course, one should yearn to love what is best, and feed the yearning by all available sources of culture; but a lying pretense of loving what we do not love, is the poorest possible basis of culture.

If you have lived among the mountains at any period of your life, or have wandered up and down those dreamy heights of the Alps, some sketch of mountain scenery, some little brown, battered *chalet*, though not of importance artistically, may yet be a charming reminder to you of other scenes, and carry such refreshment in it as will give abundant value.

If you have lived by the sea, some spirited engraving — like Haden's "Calais Pier" — that shows the flash of the water in its inks and lights, will make the murmur of the waves hang again in solace on your ear. Or, if, independent of all memories, some little charming landscape composition, whose trees you do not know, nor brook, nor mountain, and yet find so brimming in its every line with nature as to seize upon your sentiment, and win you to such serene enjoyment of tree, and cloud, and sky and flower, as you feel upon a delicious day of June — buy it; hang it on your wall; there can be no doubt that it is the picture for you.

The library, so important in many homes, as it should be in all, may have its special decorative treatment, into which the arrangement of the books will enter as a large factor. Just now there is a method, partly Eastlakeish, partly sensible, and getting to be wholly fashionable, of keeping bookshelves to a low range which shall gird the room about, leaving above them ample space for various adornment. It is a very sensible arrangement if books just suffice, or are less than sufficient, for the filling of such range of cases; but if it involve packing and doubling and cramming, to keep the fashion good, it is altogether absurd. Books fairly bound make good wall decorations in themselves, and should rise to just such height as may be needful to give full, uncramped show of their titles, every one. There should be no friends there we are ashamed of. And no colors of the paper-hangers can over-pass in piquancy, in rich charm, that assemblage of little parallelograms in gray, in brown, in black, over-crossed with fine spider lines in gold, and legends that carry the names we love always. If books have not accumulated so as to give this complete garniture, recesses may break into the shelves, with some deft turn of a light supporting arch, under which may be a bit of sculpture, or painting, or map, or historic relics. And as books accumulate and these gaps fill up, your accessories will seek other post of vantage, — all gaining, I think, somewhat by a little sense of crowding, and over-fill; the library being the one room in the house, — except it be the larder, — which will bear this over-fulness without causing æsthetic revolt.

I do not, for my own part, like the notion of keeping books cribbed and coffined under glass. They are like friends; if they cannot be used freely, they are worth little. The dust will come, and finger-marks will come. Well, let them — if only the finger-mark has given a thought-mark to match it. I cannot say but a little disarray of home-books is a good sign of familiarity, and that sort of acquaintance which makes them worshipful friends. Nay, I go farther than this, and would not give a shuttle-cock for a home-book which I might not annotate. No matter what wealth is there already, our own little halfpence may be more relished by home eyes, than the pile of gold which retains its unbroken formality.

The *usableness* of books — if I may coin the word — enters for very much into our æsthetic estimate of them as ornaments of home; and as a relief to these details about interiors, I give a glimpse or two of certain libraries which had charm by reason of their *usableness*, and which are memorable by their uses.

One, a low room, rather longer than broad, with one window looking out under forest trees through a heavy old casement upon a bight of the Hudson;

the other window looking across a little stretch of green lawn, with the view closed in by trees that shelter a glen. Furniture almost unnoticeable ; a few quaint chairs ; a few drawings endeared by this or that attaching story of friends ; books walling you in with motley bindings — Spanish, English, French, poetry, history, some fat, some slim, some unbound — a lack of uniformity that would have disgusted an upholsterer ; a long table with its equipment of writing materials, its stand for dictionaries and books of reference ; a few graceful little mementoes of wide travel scattered over it; and at the desk, in capacious chair — which is not luxurious, not artistic, save as fitness and ease give artistic character — sat, thirty years ago, the master — the amiable old gentleman — Washington Irving, whose lurking humor was always playing about an eye that I think never looked upon any human creature but with kindliness.

Another is that of a poet, who ten years since was living in the vigor of a green old age, at a home upon the shores of Long Island, and embedded amid fields and trees ; yet with the high-road from Roslyn passing near it, and sifting its dust, in summer, over patches of the lawn. There were pictures, autotypes, rich historic relics in halls and parlor ; but the library in the rear no way remarkable artistically, but full of quiet, cosy invitingness. Books of utmost variety all around the walls; an antique Franklin stove built into a chimney, that carries border of old Dutch Scripture tiles; a bay-window looking upon orchards and shrubbery, where the lithe old gentleman had intimate and most knowing ompanionship with the trees every summer's day of his life; another window looking across garden, upon a stretch of bay-water making up from the Sound; chairs that are cumbrous, even awkward, and table gauged for service only, — where was written much of his translation of Homer, and most of those snatches of poetry which had broken in upon his somewhat fiery, but always earnest political life.

Still another, where it has been sometime my fortune to go years since — was in the midst of Paris.[1] Stout walls, unpretending entrance, a plain servingman to usher you in, — no gorgeous upholstery — but plainest of hangings; no alabaster vases, no show of gilt work; at most a marble or two: great amplitude of green baize on table and floor alike; books that bear every mark of service; a portrait or two on the walls — among them that of Alexander

---

[1] The library here described, was in that old house of Guizot, not far away from the Grand Opera House — which went down — much to the historian's discomfiture — under that revision of street lines, due to the intrepid Haussmann.

Hamilton; the freshest journals and periodicals, but everywhere a most homely severity in the midst of a city crowded with art; and the master of it — Guizot: — a man, on whose word — for years together, the destinies of France hung.

I have noted these not as instances of art-decoration, but as instances where all charms lay in adaptation to, and in strong expression of the individuality of the occupants; and without this, no home interior can have any vital charm — whatever the art resources.

Yet this home expression is given largely by arrangement — far more than by quality of material. The material may be the richest and most artistic — if its disposition has only a cold precision, and wearying parallelism, and unbending order, it can never come to its cheerfullest work of welcoming, and making glad. Everybody knows what such interiors are; stiff, modish; where displacement of anything is like a dislocation: chairs in pairs and fixed; vases in pairs; pictures paired and hung in pairs, and the decorator and upholsterer at the bottom of it all — paired, and — unhung. Best of arrangement is due after all to a certain intuitive sense of the picturesque, which some people have, and others of equal culture have not. Perhaps that is all that is to be said of it. One woman will never tie a knot, but by a flirt of the fingers she gives a picturesque grace to it; she will not place a chair, but it seems *the* place; never assemble a burst of spring flowers, but it has an airy easy toss of its colors and green that is as witching as a wild-wood.

The home and its apartments should not be treated as a dead thing, where we make best arrangement of its fittings, and there leave it. It must grow in range and in expression with our necessities, and diverging, and developing tastes. The best of decorators cannot put that last finish which must come from home hands. It is a great canvas always on the easel before us — growing in its power to interest every day and year — never getting its last touches — never quite ready to be taken down and parted with. No home should so far out-top the tastes of its inmates that they cannot somewhere and somehow deck it with the record of their love and culture. It is an awful thing to live in a house where no new nail can be driven in the wall, and no tray of wild flowers, or of wood-mosses be set upon a window sill.

The ways are endless, in short, by which a house can be endowed with that home atmosphere which shall be redolent of the tastes of its inmates. The work will lie in a thousand unimportant things that cannot be named; but which by seeking, with a few main truths in your thought, you may graft to your purpose. You can never tell me with just what lifts and dashes and rests, your fingers will pass over the organ keys; but, knowing its compass, knowing the tones — knowing the result at which you aim, your fingers race away in the exaltation of that knowledge, and by a fairy legerdemain you can never explain to me, call down sweet showers of melody!

Homes and Holidays.

JUST as dividend-days brighten all stock-mongering, holidays brighten homes. A holiday that does not take a body home — either for its beginning or its end, is only a poor cousin of a holiday, that must console itself with second-hand finery. School and college holidays are of this sort, which, though they may make little bright gaps in the round of tasks and studies, with consolatory memories drifting across them, have never the flavor and the unction of a home holiday.

I foresee clearly that the tone into which I am falling here, will make of these last pages — whether they lead "indoors or out" — only a children's chapter. The little people — I have observed — always listen intently when the talk of their elders runs upon old boarding-school times, and the punishments (as to which, they prick up their ears very sharply), and the games, and the half-holidays, or the whole ones. I was describing to such a group of small people, the other night, an old New England school-room of the better sort, as it appeared fifty odd years ago; — how it was in the basement of a great ungainly building where forty or more boys lived together, with a teacher in arithmetic and geography, and a teacher in Greek and Latin, and a superintendent, and matron, and cook, and maids, and a "hired man," who astonished the boys by the great weights he could lift, and by a display of the huge biceps muscle under his red-flannel sleeve — which he obligingly rolled up from time to time, in the familiarities of evening twilight. That basement school-room — from some over-sight in construction — was subject to periodic dampness, which, in a succession of years, had left great mouldy stains upon the walls. Attempts had been made to cover these stains with lime-washes or with oil-paints, and there had been some flakings of the tissue; in consequence of all which there was afforded quite a study of color around the room — ferruginous and other — which did not take rank with the ordinary curriculum. All about this wall was a range of desks, only broken in upon where the door opened at an angle of the school-room, and again upon its further side, where a platform stood with its red table and ruler, and the chair for the master in charge. Within that outer range of desks, stretched other and broken ranges divided by alley-ways through which the master could pace up and down, over looking boy labors, and brandishing in sportive or serious mood — as circumstances favored — the red ruler.

Those desks were not of the modern machine sort ; but hand-made, ponderous, — their straight pine legs squaring three inches across, and their plank tops — innocent of paint or varnish, — showed honest ink-stains, and unctuous patches of whale-oil (no other lamp-lighting sort in those days), and goodly gashes and cuts illustrating the comparative merits of those patrons of boy cutlery — Messrs Rodgers and Wostenholm. As for class-books, we had Olney's Geography (Maltebrun not yet having come in), and Daboll's Arithmetic (with Zerah Colburn's for the young fry), and the American Preceptor, the best story in it being that of the Little Man in Black — out of Salmagundi. For Latin, there was Adams' Grammar, with Ainsworth's Dictionary, and the illustrious *Cornelius Nepos*. The Latin teacher who dealt with us was crazed on the subject of "quantities" and prosody, and he put us through such a drill in penults and antepenults, and "longs and shorts," and spondees and dactyls, as put them to a buzz in my head now — *sub tegmine Fagi* — whenever I wander under a beech tree in summer.

And it was from these surroundings, and from these books, that a holiday or half-holiday at the old school used to set us free. The Saturday afternoons, indeed, which did always belong to us, did not count for very much ; and a knotty Biblical lesson set down for the evening of that day, seemed in a degree to deflower that half-holiday of high Olympic flavors. The coming of a travelling menagerie, however, heralded long before by great colored show-bills (in a style which has since been prostituted to the glorification of crude histrionics), made a gala day for us. The elephants were indeed elephants in those times, and the giraffes were — I am positive — taller than any now known among the children of men. With what a redundant alacrity we made our best toilets on those menagerie days, and with what a superior air we marched — two abreast — through a hole in the tent, among the uninformed rustics who did not know — (as did we, through Olney, Malte-brun, and others) about the homes and habits of the strange beasts!

Other holidays came from time to time — though we thought them unfortunately rare — when some magnate of the little village was buried with a ceremonial that involved the presence of the masters: such holiday was always unheralded — save by the announcement from the platform, in these words, dearly remembered — "There'll be no school to-day, boys!"

"Whoop-la!" But we did not dare say it; yet I think that the way in which we shut our books, and let the desk-lids smack down over copybooks, and sums, and geographies, made as solid applause for the master's little speech as he ever won for much longer ones in after life.

These sudden bits of holiday put us upon our own private trails of amusement. There were a dozen — I think I could name them now — who in less than half an hour would be "sided" for a game of wicket: there were F. and F. (double F, we called them) who would walk away in meditative mood, with arms interlocked over their shoulders — playing Damon and Pythias. There was S——, one of our geniuses (of whom we had always half a dozen) who would retire to the attic — where he had special privileges; and presently in paper cap and black apron would be plunged in the intricacies of type-setting and printing; he being owner of a real press established in that privileged quarter — a much rarer toy then than now, and not so much given over to the lusts of life and of Satan. There were always one or two who had projects of "grand chances" — with prettily contrived lottery schemes for pins or marbles, with prizes of fine "alleys" or whip tops; and the shrewdest among these did, as I am credibly informed, win and lose afterward no less than four considerable estates in the countries by the Golden Gate.

There were others who gave the half — if not more — of those sudden holidays to a tramp upon the mountain that flanked the little village, — toiling through pasture lands where huckleberries grew and where sheep ran away, startled by intruding steps, — pausing for a drink from springs that bubbled from the ground, and reaching at length some veteran chestnut, under which the mosses mingled with the turf made delightful lounging place, where we lay for hours, looking down amongst the feeding cattle, and beyond upon the village plain, where the houses stood grouped under trees, and upon shining streaks of road which ran out between gray zigzag fences, till they were lost in distance and the summer haze.

And under the haze that vision of the school and of the school-fellows passes out of sight and out of mind, and other visions of home scenes come to fill its place.

—— Smoky autumn days invite to the woods, and from time to time there is great stir and excitement among the young people of a certain neighborhood about some forthcoming picnic or nutting frolic.

There is the question — first of all — of time ; it must be on a holiday of course; Wednesday would do, but Saturday is better; and on Friday, the last thing before bed, eager eyes peer into the darkness to see if the stars are shining. Then there is the great question of invitations : Master Harry must go of course, — he is a good climber and good fellow ; and Frank he must go, — who thinks of a picnic without Frank? (there are some people who are born to invitations, — without knowing the reason ; and their friends often as ignorant). Then there is little Barbara, — who shall deny little Barbara? They may have to lift her over the fences, and she may spill more nuts than she gathers; but all through life she shall go on doing the same by virtue of her sunny face and of her golden curls. Is it Lamb's mention of it that makes Barbara seem a very attractive name? Or is it some floating memory of another Barbara, — a frail little one with ruby lips for whom in boy-days we made a chair, — two of us knitting our arms together for that purpose, — and trotted off with our proud burden? I do not think we could lift Mistress Barbara now.

I could not name the half of the invited ones for our picnic ; but there are some among them whose coming have, I think, quickened a little coquetry of dress : else how happens it that Miss Floy insists upon that blue sash, so rarely brought into requisition? Is Master William to be one, Miss Floy? And Miss Floy turns squarely round, — to study the weather, — and I see only the trailing ends of the sash upon her robe of white, and cannot tell whether she be blushing or no. Master Charles, too, has planted a glowing cockade in that sailor-hat of his, which, with his white drilling trowsers and blue jacket, is very killing.

Finally, with panniers all made ready, and provisioned for a long cruise, with oranges and sandwiches and comfits, the disorderly, rollicking procession moves away. I see them winding up the hill with shouts and laughter, — now lost among the trees and again trailing over the hill pastures, and at last only a speck or two of white flitting in and out by the edge of the wood, and so vanishing into the forest shades.

Later on in the year, when snow and sunshine together have put a rosier glow into children's faces, we begin to catch sight of little fluttering side-councils and to hear very pregnant whispers, and to have intimations of secret work going forward, and of great mystery which cannot and must not be fathomed until a certain great holiday shall dawn. No money can bribe a disclosure, though it must be confessed that the little eyes look longingly, in these December times, upon such bribes as you venture to show.

There is a very earnest looking after the contents of those little portemonnaies of theirs — as if there might possibly be some little stamplet hidden within, which no eyes but eyes kindled by Christmas could discover. And if emptiness does really appear — positive — dismal emptiness, there is such a show of sighs, and such a begging, hopeful, trusting look, as is sure to win, and then to pass away in a little burst of merry laughter. Well, we have all played at that game some time in our lives. A well-filled purse on most any date in December or any other month you may be pleased to name, is very provocative of smiles.

The boys are in the right, who say that half the fun in life is in looking forward to the fun that is to come. What a jolly thing it is to think of the old grandmother's blessed start of surprise when she first catches sight, on Christmas morning, of that — what d'ye call it? — which these little granddaughters have been working upon with sly fingers, all unbeknown to her, for a month in advance! How we chuckle for weeks at thought of the glad wonderment of the old gentleman as he unfolds the wrappings, one after another, which cover some little photograph fresh as life, daintily set in its garniture of golden plush. No matter whose.

And whether we believe in toys or not, there is a storm of them gathering that will rain down on Christmas morning. Of course, it stands to reason that Tom's dancing Jack will have his head broken before nightfall: but what of that? Little Molly's wax doll will have its hair pulled off at about the same time, but this will only make a good joke against Aunt Jane, who has the same thing happening to her dear old head night after night.

But books last: and those who can't see the wisdom of breaking toys, may give books. These do not break : though the book-makers sometimes do.

And so, with toys in stock, and books and the last gifts made ready, the hum of secret merriment grows louder and louder, week by week, until eventide before the great December holiday comes flowing in fast and grandly upon the little ones all, with a great roar of mirth — subdued it may be, the while they march up the church aisle devoutly and say their Christmas prayers: and subdued still farther, the while they think of some fair fingers that wrought on last year's garlands — but not on these.

And yet I do not know but it is that old New England holiday of Thanksgiving, which for one of

New England birth has most of home associations tied up with it, and most of glee-ful memories. I know that they are very present ones :—

We all knew when it was coming; we all loved turkey — not Turkey on the map, for which we cared very little, after we had once bounded it — by the Black Sea on the east, and by something else on the other sides — but, basted turkey, brown turkey, stuffed turkey: Here was richness!

We had scored off the days until we were sure — to a recitation-mark — when it was due; well into the end of November, when winds would be blowing from the Northwest, with great piles of dry leaves all down the sides of the street, and in the angles of pasture-walls.

I cannot for my life conceive why anyone should upset the old order of things by marking it down a fortnight earlier. A man in the country wants his crops well in, and housed before he is ready to gush out with a round, out-spoken Thanksgiving: but every body knows — who knows any thing about it — that the Purple tops and the Cow-horn turnips are, nine times in ten, left out till the latter days of November, and husking not half over.

We all knew, as I said, when it was coming. We had a stock of empty flour-barrels on Town-Hill, stuffed with leaves, and a big pole set in the ground, and a battered tar-barrel, with its bung chopped out, to put on top of the pole. It was all to beat the last year's bonfire : and it did.

The country wagoners had made their little stoppages at the back door. We knew what was to come of that. And if the old cook — a monstrous fine woman, who weighed two hundred, if she weighed a pound — was brusque and would n't have us "round," we knew what was to come of that too. Such pies as hers demanded thoughtful consideration: not very large, and baked in scalloped tins, and with such a relishy flavor to them as, on my honor, I do not recognize in any pies of this generation. I bought a lithograph of one of Rubens' women once, in Antwerp, because I thought I recognized in it some resemblance to that veteran cook; albeit Rubens' charmer made fearful display of bosom — which, on my honor again, I never saw in the cook; who wore, on the contrary, a decent stuff short-gown, with a white handkerchief tied close round her neck.

The sermon on that Thanksgiving (and we all heard it) was long — unequivocally long. We boys were prepared for that too. But we could n't treat a Thanksgiving sermon as we would an ordinary one ; we could n't doze — there was too much ahead. It seemed to me that the preacher made rather a merit of holding us in check — with that basted turkey in waiting. At last though, it came to an end; and I believe Dick and I, both joined in the Doxology.

All that followed is to me now a cloud of misty and joyful expectation, until we took our places — a score or more of cousins and kinsfolk; and the turkey, and celery, and cranberries, and what-nots, were all in place.

Did Dick whisper to me as we went in: "Get next to me, old fellow"?

I cannot say. I have a half recollection that he did. But, bless me! what did any body care for what Dick said?

And the old gentleman who bowed his head and said grace — there is no forgetting him. And the little golden-haired one who sat at his left — his pet, his idol — who lisped the thanksgiving after him, shall I forget her, and the games of forfeit afterward at evening that brought her curls near to me?

These fifty years she has been gone from sight, and is dust. What an awful tide of Thanksgivings has drifted by since she bowed her golden locks, and clasped her hands, and murmured: "Our Father, we thank thee for this, and for all thy bounties!"

Who else? Well, troops of cousins — good, bad,

and indifferent. No man is accountable for his cousins, I think. Or if he is, the law should be changed. If a man can't speak honestly of cousinhood, to the third or fourth degree, what *can* he speak honestly of? Didn't I see little Floy (who wore pea-green silk) make a saucy grimace when I made a false cut at that roly-poly turkey drum-stick and landed it on the table-cloth?

There was that scamp, Tom, too, who loosened his waistcoat before he went in to dinner (I saw him do it). Didn't he make faces at me, till he caught a warning from Aunt Polly's uplifted finger?

How should I forget that good, kindly Aunt Polly — very severe in her turban, and with her meeting-house face upon her; but full of a great wealth of bon-bons and dried fruits on Saturday afternoons, in — I know not what — capacious pockets; ample, too, in her jokes, and in her laugh; making that day a great maëlstrom of mirth around her?

H—— sells hides now, and is as rich as Crœsus (whatever that may mean); but does he remember his venturesome foray for a little bit of crisp roast-pig that lay temptingly on the edge of the dish that day?

There was Sarah, too — turned of seventeen, education complete, looking down on us all — terribly learned (I know, for a fact, that she kept Mrs. Hemans in her pocket); terribly self-asserting, too : if she had not married happily, and not had a little brood about her in after years (which she did), I think she would have made one of the most terrible Sorosians of our time. At least, that is the way I think of it now, looking back across the basted turkey (which she ate without gravy) and across the range of eager Thanksgiving faces.

There was Uncle Ned — no forgetting him — who had a way of patting a boy on the head so that the patting reached clear through to the boy's heart, and made him sure of a blessing hovering over. That was the patting I liked. *That's* the sort of uncle to come to a Thanksgiving dinner; the sort that eat double filberts with you, and pay up next day by noon, with a pocket-knife or a riding-whip. Hurrah! for Uncle Ned!

And Aunt Eliza — is there any keeping her out of mind? I never liked the name much; but the face, and the kindliness which was always ready to cover — as well as she might — what wrong we did, and to make clear what good we did, make me enroll her now — where she belongs evermore — among the saints. So quiet, so gentle, so winning, making conquest of all of us, because she never sought it; full of dignity, yet never asserting it; queening it over all by downright kindliness of heart. What a wife she would have made! Heigho! How we loved her, and made our boyish love of her — a Thanksgiving!

Were there oranges? I think there were, with green spots on the peel — lately arrived from Florida. Tom boasted that he ate four. I dare say he told the truth — he looked peakèd, and was a great deal the worse for the dinner, next day, I remember.

Was there punch or any strong liquors? No — so far as my recollection now goes — there was none.

Champagne?

I have a faint remembrance of a loud pop or two, which set some cousinly curls over opposite me into a nervous shake. Yet I would not like to speak positively. Good bottled cider or pop-beer may possibly account for all the special phenomena I call to mind.

Old Madeira I have less doubt about; and it is my impression there were some stereotype gentlemen present who talked about "London Particular," and the "White Seal," and "Sercial," just as such things are talked about by stereotype people nowadays.

Was there coffee, and were there olives? Not to

the best of my recollection ; or, if present, I lose them in the glamour of mince-pies and Marlboro' puddings.

How we ever sidled away from that board when that feast was done, I have no clear conception. I am firm in the belief that thanksgiving was said at the end, as at the beginning. I have a faint recollection of a gray head passing out at the door, and of a fleece of golden curls beside him, against which I jostle — not unkindly.

Dark?

Yes, I think the sun had gone down about the time when the mince-pies faded.

Did Dick and Tom and the rest of us come sauntering in afterward when the rooms were empty, foraging for any little tid-bits of the feast that might be left — the tables showing only wreck under the dim light of a solitary candle — the long range of white cloth stretching athwart the hall like a great skeleton of the feast — lying there in state?

How we found our way with the weight of that stupendous dinner by us to the heights of Town-Hill, it is hard to tell. But we did, and when our barrel-pile was fairly ablaze, we danced like young satyrs round the flame — shouting at our very loudest when the fire caught the tar-barrel at the top, and the yellow pile of blaze threw its lurid glare over hill, and houses, and town, and the far-away bay, and wooded hills.

Afterward I have recollection of an hour or more in a snug square parlor, which is given over to us youngsters and our games: dimly lighted, as was most fitting; but a fire upon the hearth flung out a red glory on the floor and on the walls.

Was it a high old time, or did we only pretend that it was?

Didn't I know little Floy, in that pea-green silk, with my hands clasped round her waist, and my eyes blinded — ever so fast? Didn't I give Dick an awful pinch in the leg, when I lay *perdu* under the sofa in another one of those tremendous games?

Didn't the door that led into the hall show a little open gap, from time to time — old faces peering in, looking very kindly in the red fire-light flaring on them? And didn't those we loved best look oftenest? Don't they always?

Well, well — we were fagged at last: little Floy in a snooze before we knew it; Dick, pretending not to be sleepy, but gaping in a prodigious way. But the romps and the fatigue made sleep very grateful when it came at last: yet the sleep was very broken: the turkey and the nuts had their rights, and bred stupendous Thanksgiving dreams. What gorgeous dreams they were to be sure!

I seem to dream them again to-day.

Once again, — I see the old, revered gray head, bowing in utter thankfulness, with the hands clasped.

Once again, — over the awful tide of intervening years — so full, and yet so short — I seem to see the shimmer of *her* golden hair — an aureole of light blazing on the borders of boyhood: "*For this, and all thy bounties, our Father, we thank thee.*"

THE END.

www.ingramcontent.com/pod-product-compliance
Lightning Source LLC
Chambersburg PA
CBHW031329230426
43670CB00006B/281